MOM
to MOM . . .

MOM
to MOM ...

STAGES OF MOTHERHOOD
REVEALED

JESSICA RAISTRICK, LCSW

Mom to Mom . . . Stages of Motherhood Revealed
Published by Inner Truth Consulting

Copyright 2025 by Jessica Raistrick

ISBN 979-8-218-61604-5

Cover Design- Barton Creative Co.
Book Interior Design Iram Allam

www.innertruthconsulting.com

Printed in the United States of America

1 3 5 7 9 10 8 6 4 2

CONTENTS

ACKNOWLEDGMENTS

I want to begin by saying thank you . . .

Thank you for your interest in reading this book. My hope is that you'll discover moments where you can see yourself, gain education, and understand that we all experience motherhood differently. If there are sections where you don't see yourself, perhaps you'll see a friend or colleague instead. I recognize that every mother finds different joys and struggles at various stages of her journey through motherhood. Therefore, please feel free to take what resonates with you, discover ways to better support yourself or other mothers, and leave behind what doesn't suit you. Our experiences matter—all of them. With this understanding, I hope we can support each other, no matter where we are on our path.

This is to all the moms out there who choose love and courage over fear every day. This book has truly inspired me, and I am grateful to all who contributed their nuggets of wisdom to this process. I admire you, honor you, and respect you.

Last but not least, to my mom, I wouldn't be the mother I am today without you. Thank you for showing me what it means to be a healthy mother, find balance, and love with all my heart. You've shown me what it means to love unconditionally as a mother and a woman. With that as my foundation, I feel equipped to climb the highest mountains with those I love.

INTRODUCTION

Becoming a mom is a journey that some may dream of, have a deep-seated desire for, or find themselves contemplating at various stages of life. For other women, it comes as an unexpected surprise, prompting deep reflection about whether to embark on this life-changing adventure. No matter how you arrived here, it's clear that the shelves are brimming with books on how to be the perfect parent—a goal that we all know is unattainable. Yet, we strive to minimize our mistakes and do our best for our children.

Despite the plethora of parenting guides, there's a noticeable gap in the literature: books that delve into the emotional stages we experience as mothers and the tumultuous roller coaster we ride as our children grow. This realization has inspired me to create a book that not only resonates with women but also brings a sense of humor to the often chaotic world of parenting. It's for those times when we feel clueless, terrified, and like a hot mess. My hope is that this book will provide a sense of connection, a laugh, and a reminder that we're all in this together, navigating the beautiful, complicated journey of motherhood.

Women need more honesty about being a mother, and all it entails. I notice how much women monitor what they say about their children or how they feel for fear of being judged. "Mom guilt" is also a genuine thing. Speaking the truth about how hard it can be to be a mother can invoke a great deal of guilt, causing women to shy away from it for feeling like they should think this is the best thing ever and that they are flawed human beings if they say otherwise. After I had my son, I remember having friends who acted as if being a mom was the best thing in the world. All I wanted to say was, "Yes, it is a wonderful gift, and it's also hard as hell, so stop pretending like you're not exhausted and want to cry alone sometimes."

Since having a child, being a therapist, and becoming a stepmother, I have spent several years helping parents and children and helping myself to better understand the struggles and stages of motherhood we go through as women. As I have engaged in these experiences, I have come up with the seven stages of motherhood relating to mothers and their experiences. I hope you can find a connection and relate to these stages to glean some insight into what's to come.

My last goal in writing this book is to enlighten you with techniques and skills to help you stay sane and have a positive motherhood experience. I typically hear women say the phrase, "If I only knew then what I know now, I would have done things differently." I hope you will take some of this information and utilize it to the best of your ability so you can experience the joys of motherhood and better manage the hardships. To that end, I have also included at the end of each chapter some "food for thought" as well as responses from women of all walks of life to myriad questions in an effort to share their nuggets of wisdom about this journey for a deeper societal connection. Lastly, you will find a question that encourages you to check in with yourself and journal some notes in those brief moments you have to yourself. The earlier you start to practice these skills, the more apt you will be to use them at each stage. They will help to strengthen your confidence in the decisions you make as a mother. Each step you take builds on the next.

I hope to help you walk with confidence each step of the way.

CHAPTER 1

WHAT THE *BLEEP* AM I DOING?

Stage 1–Pregnancy Up Through Birth to Six Months

Pregnancy Phase

Remember the day you found out you were pregnant? Regardless of whether this was planned, or an accident, fear and unease lurk under the surface of this amazing miracle that has just occurred. Getting pregnant is a miracle, considering how all the "stars need to align" to create this wonderful little being in your body. Once the excitement of this news sinks in, the nervousness soon arrives along with it, as we start to explore thoughts of "When can I tell people?" "What if I miscarry?" "If I tell people too soon and something happens, then I have to tell everyone the bad news. How do I want to tell everyone? Should I google the best ways to tell my parents? Or put the sonogram in a card? Will I breast- or bottle-feed? Will I have an all-natural birth or have an epidural? Should I have the baby in the hospital or home birth?" And on . . . and on . . . and on. That's not even considering the endless amounts of books women tend to search like *What to Expect When You're Expecting*, and our desire to make sure we eat exactly the way we are supposed to, stay within the proper weight range, use pregnancy as a rationalization to eat everything we wouldn't usually allow ourselves because we "have a craving," or deprive ourselves because we are worried we won't be able to lose the baby weight after they arrive and be in maternity clothes forever.

Phew!

So, how do we handle all our fears and worries? We try to control as many variables as humanly possible: our environment and sometimes our spouses. We all have those moments when we think, "Wow, this is really happening." At the beginning of our pregnancy, it is still surreal as our bodies haven't changed much, and we don't feel anything inside. Come the second trimester, our bodies start to change, and this can be a time of truly understanding what it feels like to have a lack of control. What I mean by this is our bodies are changing, and there isn't much we can do about it. Our children will get their needs met come hell or high water—and our bodies will take care of their growth process before it takes care of our own. When you think about it, it is the first time we need to ensure we take extra good care of ourselves. Still, we are spending so much time worrying about our unborn child that we neglect our needs to focus on theirs. This is interesting as it becomes a lifelong pattern that we, as women, must autocorrect at some point.

Remember, if the plane is going down, we need to put on our oxygen masks before we can put on our child's mask—a concept that many women have struggled with throughout history. So, to all those women who are reading this and are pregnant right now, you do you! Please start thinking about your needs and taking care of them; it's good practice for what's to come.

What's coming is your last trimester and the reality of how it feels to be uncomfortable in your own skin. We all know the end of our pregnancy is super exciting, as this little bun we have been baking is about to show up and we can't wait to meet them. The excitement of what they will look like, how they will feel, and the anticipation of life's changes are all-encompassing. Simultaneously, we feel like the Goodyear Blimp—with a waddle—and getting comfortable is a nonstarter, no matter what position we find ourselves in. There aren't enough body pillows in the world to sleep soundly through the night anymore, and if we have to wake up to pee one more time, we might kick our partner, so they have to suffer with us. After all, misery definitely loves company. You know, we have all had the thought, "Why do *they* get to have a good night's sleep? This is horseshit."

So . . . we are nearing the finish line, and our to-do list is still pretty long: Finish the baby's room; do I really like the name we picked out? And how many ways can other kids make fun of their name? I still have to pack my hospital bag; did I get everything I needed at my baby shower? Or is there still some online shopping that needs to happen? Is our house big enough? Who will take care of our pets while I'm in the hospital? I plan to breastfeed, but what if I can't or they don't latch—will that make me a bad mom? What if I must have a C-section? I hope everything goes smoothly; how will this feel? Am I doing all-natural? Does work have all the required paperwork? Do we have enough money so I can take my maternity leave, or will I have to go back early? I wish my partner made more money because leaving my baby to return to work sounds awful. Do I want anyone besides my partner in the delivery room with me? How do I politely tell everyone what my wishes are with this process?

Yes, that list is exhausting and makes me tired just reading it. The excitement and adrenaline rush are at an all-time high, and since you can't sleep, it's the perfect playground for overthinking. Repeat after me, "Deep breath. I will get through this, one step at a time."

How do you get through this phase of stage 1?

FOOD FOR THOUGHT

- Know that you won't do this perfectly, and that's okay.

- Understand that too much information is not helpful. Manage your anxiety by speaking with your OB-GYN and trusted sources; avoid going to Google for all of your information.

- Learn healthy ways to manage your fears. Trying to control everything will work temporarily, but it is not a practical solution in the long haul.

- Listen to your body; if it's telling you it's tired, then rest. If it's hurting, try to understand why and what you need to do to support yourself.

- Make lists of what you must do, and work with your partner to address the list together. If you start trying to be Wonder Woman now, you are setting up a dynamic that is not sustainable when having a family. Check items off the list, as it provides a beautiful sense of accomplishment.

- Make sure you and your partner clearly communicate about what you want the delivery to look like, including who will be in the room, who can visit in the hospital, and whether you want visitors when the baby first comes home. Make sure you are on the same page and support each other because family members can be challenging no matter how much you love them.

You don't have to breastfeed if it doesn't feel right. Don't give in to peer pressure about how to feed your child. Whatever you choose will be right!

Subsection: The Baby Is Here Phase

I can't believe I just had a million people looking at my vagina, and I couldn't control my bowels. Will my partner ever want to have sex with me again? Why didn't anyone tell me about any of this in all the stuff I read about what happens during childbirth? Oh, right, and now I'm scared I'll be responsible for this little human being . . . forever!

We all experience this incredible moment when our baby is born, and we share this beautiful exchange with our partner as we both take part in this moment of creating life. It is truly magnificent and one of the best gifts we can experience. To feel our child's skin against ours awakens the soul in a way you never could have imagined. Exhausted and adrenaline-filled, we soak in this moment the best we can while emotionally and physically exhausted. As the medical team whisks away our child to conduct testing and evaluations, we are told to rest, and yet we are still trying to process what just happened and how this child will be in our care soon. The first night in the hospital with our child, whether they are next to us in the same room or somewhere else in the hospital, is angst-producing at best. Yet it also provides a sense of safety because if we have any questions, we know that highly qualified people are available to help us at any given moment. We all wish we knew that the goal at this juncture was to ensure we were absorbing as much of their knowledge as possible by taking notes. Soon, we will be heading home with this incredible being, and we think we have a clue as to what we are in for, but that's a good laugh at best.

The day has arrived, and we are expected to take our child home. We have packed up all our things, including our child, and the car seat has been installed and checked by the nursing staff. We are off. This is probably the safest car ride you will ever take in your life as you and your partner are too scared to take any risks and damage the precious cargo you now have in the back seat. You pull into the driveway and think to yourself, "I can't believe this is happening! I'm so excited and have no idea what I am doing," all at the same time. As you walk into the house, you think, "I can do this . . . but wait—what do I do now?" You start to navigate life in this whole new way; things you have never thought about before now become things you think about. You want to be near this little creation as much as possible, yet you are so exhausted that you are on overdrive and thinking of everything you need to do. As you settle in and start to use all of the great gifts you received at your baby shower, you soon encounter moments where the baby is crying, and you genuinely have no idea why, or they make a weird face, and you fear something is wrong and then think to yourself, "How on earth will I know something is wrong if they can't talk!"

The first few days and nights at home can be overwhelming as you realize this isn't like babysitting; this is the real deal. You fight the urge to call your pediatrician every five minutes to ensure the baby is okay and you are doing all the right things. You're excited to have help and are simultaneously overwhelmed with all the opinions flying around about what you should do and how you should do it. When this happens, it is crucial to check in with yourself about what you need and find a way to communicate it. You have added a new role in your life, which changes all others and can make other roles feel blurry in the beginning.

Be kind to your mother and mother-in-law; they have the best intentions, even though they may sometimes annoy you. The truth is, they want to be included and support you in whatever way they can. They are proud and in awe of this new life that has just been brought into the world. Regardless of how you feel about your mother-in-law, this is their grandchild, and the more you resist their participation, the more challenging your life will become.

Take time to converse with your partner about finding a balance that feels good to both of you regarding visitors and support. Remember, opinions are like assholes; everyone has one. You don't have to do what everyone says. Still, you can benefit from some fabulous kernels of wisdom if you allow yourself to be open and listen. Another thing to think about is that having your parents or in-laws watch your child for daycare can be extremely tricky. Now, I know it's pretty appealing financially (who doesn't love free), but with free care comes a feeling that they have more of a right to let you know what they think your child needs and how to handle it. I have seen this play out in a multitude of ways, but the main impact is you feeling like you're not a great mom, pissed that they have the gall to tell you what to do, and feeling defensive. Having a loved one watch your child one or two days a week is far more manageable, and it feels less intrusive than when they watch your child as a full-time job.

The other piece to keep in mind is that socialization is a beautiful thing for children. You will be in awe of how much they learn and advance in a structured setting, and you have nothing to feel guilty about. At the end of the day, we all need to accept that no one will take care of our child the way we do, but that doesn't mean they are incapable of still doing a good job. This is one of your first experiences of letting go as a parent; it's hard but will be the first of many experiences of letting go, so it's better to start embracing it now. One of my favorite things to do when I returned to work was to take a day off when my part-ner was at work and my son was in daycare, so I could do whatever my little heart desired without someone needing me. I promise it's a treasured feeling, and there's less guilt involved when you know you pay for daycare.

As you navigate the early stages of motherhood, it is okay not to hold your child every second of the day. That feeling you must always hold them is something important for you to be aware of, and what the emotion is behind that need for you. We need to be willing to ask ourselves at different points in our mothering careers, "Do I need to hold them constantly?" Or, "Why can't I let them be in the swing instead of holding them all the time?" This is a time when our learned attachment shows up from our upbringing. We can see in ourselves where we have learned to attach to others or detach from others and what may trigger this within us. Our ability to explore ourselves and why we are making the choices we make as a mom will be paramount in our experience and how our children experience us.

As you learn to navigate being home with your newborn, it's natural to wonder what you will do all day—or if you will go stir-crazy because you have been talking goo-goo ga-ga for twelve hours straight. It's surprising how much time this sweet little being can take up in addition to the chores and tasks of daily living. Whether it's your partner or you returning to work, it's a significant change that creates varying degrees of fear or stress. Please know that, no matter what, you will get through it; I promise. During these massive life changes, it is essential to be kind to yourself and know that not everything will get done, and that's okay. Your ability to talk with your partner ahead of time regarding your roles as a couple and as parents is crucial. There may be roles you both engaged in during the early stages of your relationship that may no longer fit now that you are parents. Or you may have decided against engaging in a specific role over time—that you hate it and want to make a change. Now is the perfect time for those changes. Talk about how things are working or not working. These conversations are vital to the survival of your marriage and the health of your parenting. Our adaptability as a whole in our relationships is something my children have taught me repeatedly. Adaptability is essential as we realize that we can't control everything, and we don't know how to do this perfectly. When we can adapt and adjust course as needed, it provides us with a flow in life instead of bucking up against a wall at every turn. What may work now may not work in a year, and that's okay if you are willing to acknowledge that and problem-solve to move forward in a healthy way.

Speaking of working—at this time, it is imperative that you create time and space for your partner. Whether this is date night or cuddle time on the couch when the baby goes to bed, making time for your relationship is extremely important. In these early stages, couples sometimes stop communicating about everything else in the world but their child, and as a result, it can create a disconnect that can lead to resentment if it's not addressed. By nature, when a child comes into the picture, the primary caregiver is the one who feels torn between roles. In contrast, their partner feels left out and often lonely. Most couples struggle to talk about this as they think they should just be happy they have this child; they don't want to upset each other or are too tired to deal with anything else. You will never regret checking in and making time for your partner. Checking in can look like asking your partner, "How do you feel we are doing as a couple?" or "Am I meeting your needs?" A healthy marriage equals a healthy home.

How to Get Through the Baby Coming Home

Food for Thought

- Ask questions of the medical team at the hospital. They are there for a reason, so soak up all the information you can before you leave. Take advantage of their cumulative experience; they have the knowledge you need.

- You need to make sure you sleep. I know you're thinking, "Are you insane?" No, I'm not. Sleep is scarce, so get it when you can. You don't have to clean the house every time the baby naps; when they nap, you nap.

- You need to acknowledge your nervousness and fear with someone safe in your life. Pretending you can do everything and have it all under control will only hurt you in the long run. The better you can honor your stress, the better you will be able to care for yourself so you are the best mom you can be.

- If there are people in your life who want to support you, they need to know how you want that support—get over yourself and ask for it. There is no shame in saying, "I'm exhausted and want time alone or a date with my partner."

- Check in with your partner and ask them what they need. They are going through their own radical shift in life. Even though you may feel you are doing the larger share, they may feel lost, pushed aside, lonely, or scared. Schedule date night on a regular basis.

- Don't ignore that postpartum depression is a real thing, and if you are feeling sad, detached, irritable, not wanting to care for your child, or lack joy, make sure you talk to your OB-GYN, your partner, or a therapist. Don't let it go. Hormones are potent forces, and they can change our moods in a heartbeat. I want to reassure you that this is not a flaw in you; this is your body trying to figure out how to readjust after the baby is born, and you deserve to feel better. Seek support; there is no shame in feeling this way, and *it's not your fault*.

So, now that this fabulous little bundle of joy is home, you are continually learning to adapt to this massive shift in your life. The reality of finances can show up when you start to determine if it's fiscally beneficial for you to return to work, or when you do return to work and you must consider the cost of daycare. It can be very easy to get lost in the financial responsibilities presented when we have children. The USDA website states that it costs nearly a quarter of a million dollars to raise a child to the age of eighteen. I remember thinking when I read this, "Are you shitting me . . . ? I have three-quarters of a million dollars living in my household!" I also thought, "If people knew this before having children, they would be extremely discouraged to take the plunge." If you haven't talked about finances and how they will change when children come, please do. If possible, speak with a financial advisor to help you manage your resources effectively. Depriving your retirement for your children is not beneficial to anyone. I know it's tough to fight the urge to spoil our children and ensure they have everything they want and need, but that's not real in all our experiences as moms.

Lastly, I want to be honest and share with you that there is some grieving that starts to take place when the baby comes home. There's that difficult moment when you realize it isn't about you anymore. When people come over or call, they ask about the baby for the most part, which can start the feeling of "What about me? I just pushed this watermelon out, and I'm still recovering!" We all go through it, and some manage this grief better than others. This is the beginning of our journey to ensure that we are taking care of ourselves and our needs while nurturing our family. It's okay to tell your partner after the baby comes home that you need something to be about you or you need them to do something sweet.

This reminds me of when I worked with Natalia, a young mother with a newborn at home. She had come into my office wondering if she was struggling with the changes of having a new baby at home. As we processed some of the emotions she was experiencing, one of them was her desire to be seen by her husband even though they had this wonderful addition to their family. She was grieving the loss of his undivided attention and affection, fearful she wouldn't get it back. We explored what she specifically missed that her husband would do and how to communicate this with him. After we role-played a scenario, she was tasked with the homework of trying to have this conversation before her next session. When she returned a few weeks later, she smiled as she walked through the door and said, "I did it," as she beamed with pride at expressing her need and having her partner meet it. If you struggle to speak up about your needs, I want to encourage you to dig deep and check in with yourself. If you start ignoring your needs, it will be really hard to reconnect with yourself down the line. Don't lose you!

To illustrate this point, I talked to a bunch of moms and asked them this question: How have you taken care of yourself as a mother who is also a woman? I think their answers to this question will resonate. What you will see is that taking care of yourself looks different for each person.

One mother stated, "Learning to take care of myself is an ongoing journey. But I love spa days, of course! The best self-care for me is taking time to hang out with a close girlfriend. This is truly soul recharging." Another mother said,

"I would carve out time to be alone, to exercise, to take walks, and always carve out time to talk to my friends. It was good for my mental health to have time for myself and to be able to ask myself what I needed when I was taking a break."

When asking this question, I noticed how seeking support from our loved ones and friends was big on the list. Reading the responses truly supported the phrase "it takes a village." While some women spoke of connection with their friends as a good bucket filler, others would express date nights with their partners or having a flexible work schedule, which made it easier to schedule some alone time. Other mothers have expressed how utilizing their community of loved ones or professionals has helped them to see they aren't alone and they aren't "crazy."

One mother expressed, "I exercise, lunch with my girlfriends once a month, and I have a job I'm interested in," while another mom said, "I didn't always in the beginning, but I have learned that I need to do things that make me happy such as getting my nails done, dinner with friends, massages, and exercise." For those who have struggled to care for themselves, here is what they have said: "I feel like I'm usually last on my priority list, but I do try to maintain caring for myself through therapy and staying in touch with nature"; and "I haven't taken good care of myself. Since I haven't, anxiety and depression has crept in and caused issues with my mental health. I also didn't have the support from my husband to take time for myself." This is not an uncommon theme I have witnessed in speaking with different mothers and learning of their experiences. Mothers who have less support at home tend to appear anxious and overwhelmed by all that's on their plate on a regular basis.

Lastly, in speaking with some women who were grandmothers and removed from the trials and tribulations of early motherhood, they appeared able to look at mothering from an elevated stance by stating, "I don't think I did anything specifically; it was a role that I always enjoyed, and found growth in. I enjoy both kids and teenagers. I was fortunate enough to stay home and not have to work for a period of time. When they became teenagers, I would exercise; I just didn't think of it in those terms." Another said, "I have taken care of myself as a woman and a mother by getting therapy when I need it, going out for dinner with friends, and occasionally traveling on my own—without my family—so I can get in touch with who I am again." This last statement seems to encompass the beauty of mind, body, and spirit as we walk this path: "Being a mother is not what defines me, though I love the role. To be effective in any relationship, I have learned I must care for myself. You cannot give what you do not have. All aspects of care were essential. For my mind—I kept learning and growing intellectually. I sought friendships that encouraged me to grow as well as play. For my body—I ate healthy, exercised, and engaged in holistic care. Emotionally—I found the tools and help to heal from my past traumas. Spiritually— This was my top priority, and as I sought to know and deepen my relationship with my God, the care of mind and body followed."

MOTHERHOOD DAILY CHECKLIST

1. Get sufficient sleep (at least multiple consecutive hours).
2. Eat three meals.
3. Shower every day.
4. Connect with someone outside of your child.
5. Take at least twenty minutes to do something that makes you feel good.

Action Step

How can you take care of yourself as you continue with this new role of motherhood?

Notes

_____
_____
_____
_____
_____
_____
_____
_____
_____
_____
_____
_____
_____
_____
_____
_____
_____
_____
_____
_____
_____
_____
_____
_____
_____
_____
_____

CHAPTER 2

I'M SO EXHAUSTED I CAN'T THINK

Second Stage–From Infant to Toddler

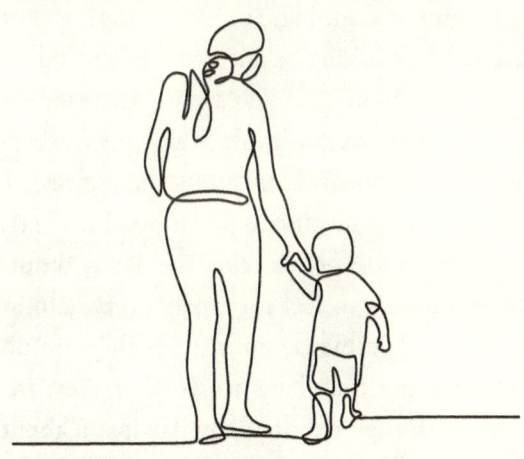

Whether you are a "stay-at-home mom" or a "working mom," what you are now realizing is that you may be the keeper of all logistics concerning your life, your child's life, and the life of your family. This is a huge responsibility. Some of us fall into this position, and some of us take it on willingly. What I mean is that we can easily become the person who takes on most of the mental load in planning, scheduling, and running interference when things don't go well. This is a big job and requires great coordination, focus, and discipline. I was the mother who ran into daycare a minute before they closed to get my son and felt awful that I was the last one there—yet so proud I could make it there before they closed. Don't ask me how this happens, but it does. There can be this looming feeling of always trying to beat the clock. You are running to daycare, running errands, running to work, running to the gym, running to dinner, running, running, running. Just when you thought you couldn't be any more exhausted than you already are, you realize that you are so exhausted you can't think, finish a sentence, or speak (which my husband loves when those rare opportunities present themselves). This is a stage when you are adjusting to parenthood while trying to figure out how to just get through the day without falling asleep or crying. It can feel extremely overwhelming, and most women feel immense guilt when they are not with their child because they have to work or they are home all the time with their children and daydream about being somewhere else. Either way you slice the pie, guilt can be an overwhelming emotion for moms at this stage.

I'll never forget when Mary started coming to see me because she felt like she wasn't doing anything well—and felt guilt no matter what she did. I remember her saying, "I have to leave for work, and I don't want to leave him at daycare, and then when I pick him up from daycare, all I think about is how many things I have to do when I get home, and it leaves me no time to spend with my son or my husband. This feeling sucks!" We took some time to explore how she felt like she was always thinking about what she needed to do, and as a result, she wasn't present, which fueled her feelings of guilt. We explored the narrative she has in her head about what a "good mom" is and whether or not that is a realistic expectation to place upon herself. We also dove further into "What happens when we feel guilty?"

We often read articles and listen to podcasts to figure out how we can do things better and to end a certain feeling we are having. At times, we send ourselves so far down the rabbit hole that we end up being filled with more guilt because we read things that we didn't even think of—and feel badly it didn't come to us first. Mom guilt is extremely common, and if a mother tells you they haven't ever felt guilty, they are lying. It's okay to feel guilt, and it's even more important to learn how to let it come—and let it go. Letting it go requires you to feel the emotion first and allow it to just be what it is. Once you acknowledge it and where you feel it in your body, you should take the next step of naming/speaking it to someone you love and trust. As we allow this emotion to flow through us, we allow it to do just that: flow through and not set up shop in our body. When we try to ignore this feeling—or stuff it down—it will rear its ugly head later, with more intensity.

Another important thing to remember when you feel your "mom guilt" is to be easy on yourself. I want you to hear me reminding you that you didn't take any classes to become a mom; you had no idea how this was going to go, and yet you still had the courage to take this journey. You show up every day, and that is truly beautiful. So show yourself some grace.

You are an amazingly powerful being. You are the apple of your child's eye and the wind beneath their wings; how *incredible* is that? This gift you have to create and shape the life of another is breathtaking. And as a result, we need to refocus our energy on what we do well, not where we are lacking. I tell people all the time, "I'm a therapist, and I'm sure my kids will be in therapy someday talking about how I messed them up because I want to talk about everything." The sooner we accept that we aren't going to do this perfectly, the better parents we will become.

To experience this feeling of acceptance, you need to stop comparing yourself when you see your other friends parenting or when you talk about parenting techniques. Comparing parenting styles is a conversation that typically goes nowhere. It's like talking about religion and politics at the dinner table . . . don't do it. Every child is different, with unique variables that impact who they are and who they ultimately become. Parenting styles that work for one of your children may not work for another, even though they are being raised by the same parents in the same environment. You and your partner are the "experts" on your children, as you observe their behavior while learning all of their little idiosyncrasies. It is this knowledge that is helpful in guiding your parenting style. When you are feeling insecure about what to do in a given situation, that is okay. Take time and explore the options, talk with your partner at length, and gain insight from others you respect as parents. You will know what feels right if you take the time to listen to your intuition. Gut instinct is real—and "mommy gut" is even more intense. When we hone our intuition, it creates a mommy gut that is unstoppable.

My client Leslie struggled with hearing her mommy gut at this stage and so she worked hard to explore how she was blocking her ability to hear her intuition. What we realized was that her anxiety from having a child increased tenfold, and as a result, she started trying to exert influence over everything in her surroundings to feel an internal sense of control. This was because she was feeling so utterly insecure in this new role of motherhood. We took some time to look at how controlling her environment in the past worked to manage her worries. But this coping skill was no longer working because she had too many things she was thinking about—or needing to do—at any given time to be able to manage on her own. We processed the concept of intuition in-depth and discussed the above techniques to help her understand how intuition is extremely important when it comes to knowing the difference between fear and gut instinct as we watch our children develop. What I mean is that fear occurs when we think our children aren't reaching their milestones or we see our friends' children doing something that our child isn't doing at the same age.

This can be challenging for some, and I want to honor that fear. I also want to reassure you that not everything our children do means they need to see a therapist or that they are immeasurably screwed up. It can be easy to catastrophize and seek help too quickly when, in reality, it's just a phase. It's healthy to be aware of milestones and just as healthy to remain patient at times to just watch and see how things play out. Not everything has to be addressed right away; give yourself time to watch and feel what is going on instead of overthinking it. An example of this is if you have a little boy who wants to play with dolls or a little girl who likes playing with trucks. This does not automatically determine that they will struggle with gender issues or sexuality. It's a stage wherein they are pure, and simply exploring. For some children, when you look back, this may be where you had a feeling as to what their sexuality was going to be, and yet for others it was purely a time of discovery. Regardless of what is happening, stay grounded and allow them to explore; it's healthy and innocent.

How This Stage Impacts Your Intimate Partnership . . .

Mothers . . . if you think all of this won't impact your intimate life . . . it will. Whether you are a single mom trying to date or in a committed relationship/marriage, this new chapter in life tests the strength of the relationships we are in. Whenever we bring someone into a dynamic or take someone out, the dynamic shifts whether we want it to or not. Adding a member or multiple members to your family is going to change the vibe of the household and the time you spend with your partner. If you are raising your child alone, having been a single mom for a period of time, I can say that this stage also changes our ability to find the time and energy to date—or even make time for our new love. Sometimes the last thing we want to do (if we are single or in a relationship) is to get all dressed up and have a rockin' night out. It takes everything in us to wake up in the morning, and trying to be romantic can sound even more exhausting. The beauty in all this change is that you have choices, no matter what stage you are in, and each day you wake up you can do it differently.

Being that stage 2 is quite angst-producing—from worrying about your child starting to walk and bang their head on sharp corners to becoming exhausted because you are trying to get your child to sleep through the night and it's not working—the person who gets the short end of the stick is usually your partner. Like it or not, this is a reality you face and one that is imperative to be mindful of. At this stage of my son's development, I can honestly say I fell from grace repeatedly because I didn't take care of myself the way I needed to (hence why I am writing this book).

Okay, let's get into the good stuff. The ways in which your marriage may be influenced by this stage of motherhood are as follows:

- Because you are exhausted, typically, at times you may start to take out your feelings on your partner and use them as your dartboard—unintentionally, of course.

- Your fears may heighten as your child grows in leaps and bounds and you aren't sure what to do. You want to look to your partner for support, but they don't know what is going on either, so you both stare at each other until someone pretends they have some confidence in how to handle the situation, and you go from there.

- The argument of who "does more" is very real and extremely frustrating. This can show up in a multitude of ways, and it can be quite damaging to a relationship if not spoken of during its infancy. Couples I have seen and many people I know inevitably get into multiple disagreements about the tasks and chores that need to be done and who feels like they are doing the lion's share. It is an exhausting discussion on top of managing all the other day-to-day things just to stay afloat.

- At times you may feel extremely unattractive and uncomfortable in your own skin because it has stretched and moved in ways you never thought possible.

- *Sex?* That's right, your partner still wants to have sexual relations with you, and it can be the last thing on your mind, especially after you have been peed and thrown up on multiple times throughout that day. As much as you love this new bundle of joy that you are caring for, they require a lot of attention, and the last thing you may feel like doing is giving attention to anyone else in the world because all you want to do is just go to bed.

- Your partner feels neglected in some way, shape, or form. No matter how hard you try to make nice dinners, have the house clean, buy him nice clothes, etc., your partner may yearn for the way it used to be when they had your complete, undivided attention. Getting them to admit that is not an easy feat, as they feel just as guilty for feeling that way as you do for not wanting them to touch you. Also, you may want to be left alone, but when you are, you don't know what to do with yourself.

How to Handle and Possibly Prevent the Above Concerns

FOOD FOR THOUGHT

Get some sleep, rest, and downtime. You need to schedule this, or it won't happen; trust me, I know. Take time off from work when no one is around. Ask your partner to do baby duty a night or two a week so you aren't doing it all on your own.

- Fear can sneak up on us all relatively quickly and with a vengeance. It is essential that you are aware of your fears and anxieties and how they show up in your life right now. I'm a fan of writing lists—start with a list of your fears or what is stressing you out at this phase.

Then, next to that list, note how these fears show up in how you react to situations throughout the day. This is an excellent start to raising awareness of your feelings, which will help start the conversation with your partner.

- When you feel yourself taking mental notes about how little your partner does, or you are having a conversation in your head about how much you're doing, and you think, "I wish I could get some help," you know that resentment is starting to build. When this happens, it's like a toxic death to a relationship. This is your body and mind's way of telling you that you are on overload and need to reassess and slow down (I know you think that's a joke—and there is no way slowing down is an option—but it is an option if you are willing to be uncomfortable). When these feelings creep in, you need to talk to your partner about how overloaded you feel and check in about your roles again. Discuss what is and is not working at this stage in your parenthood and relationship. These conversations will be the glue that keeps you sane, so don't take them for granted.

- I promise you that you are not alone adjusting to your new body. It feels foreign and takes quite some time to get used to. It's okay, and you will find a way to start to love your body even though it's not the same as it was. Remember, this is the same body that allowed you to create a miracle. Your body will never be the same and yet there is this beautiful liberation in knowing that you created life, and no one can touch that. Take some time to get a massage, exercise, do yoga, or play a sport. Enjoy a little retail therapy, and instead of forcing yourself to fit back into your old clothes, buy some new ones that complement the beautiful new figure you are trying out. Consider trying a new hairstyle; the world is your oyster, so take advantage of it. As we age, we go through several different "shedding" processes, and this is the first of many, so buckle up, buttercup; the ride has just begun.

- It can be challenging to switch from mom mode to sexy partner mode. All of the things I have just expressed are going to help you to feel attractive and even allow you to want to be sexually intimate with your partner. If we don't give to ourselves, we will have nothing to offer to our partner. Make sure you schedule date nights on a regular basis and do not talk about your child. Be silly, do something "crazy," and try to have fun with each other. Laughter is truly the best medicine, and it will help you reconnect, which is the most important thing for your relationship and child.

- Being aware of how our partner behaves when feeling neglected is key. Some regress and you feel like you have another child in the house; others may shut down emotionally and stop communicating, while others may spend more time out of the house than at home. Sometimes, it's hard to see past the behavior, but once you can, you can reconnect. Yes, you are going through a considerable change in your life, and it's important to remember that your partner is, too, just in a different way. It is essential to find the time and energy to focus on what they do to help and acknowledge them for that.

- Schedule time alone, even if it's only for an hour. You need time to be alone to do what brings you joy. If we don't refill our cup regularly, our tank will empty quickly, and everyone will have to pay. One of my favorite things to do is to "kick" everyone out of the house, turn on my music, and poke around. For me that can mean getting laundry done, writing, giving myself a facial, or reading. Whatever it is, I enjoy having time when no one needs my attention, and I can focus all my energy on myself and what I need. It's a beautiful thing and one we should never take for granted. If you don't have a partner or your partner isn't available to help give you this space, make sure to utilize your community. When I was alone with my son, I would connect with other single mothers, and we would help each other out by watching our kids so we could each get time and space to take care of ourselves or maybe have a coffee date. It takes a village!

As a result of your child growing and developing so quickly at this stage, it can be enough to make your head spin and your heart fill with pure love. You may experience moments where you literally can't get enough of them. At other times, if you could, you would inhale them. Then there are times when you wonder where your child went and when they will come back. I remember hearing horror stories and tidbits of advice on the terrible twos, but honestly, my son didn't go through that. So here I was in emotional preparation for my son to become the "spawn of the devil," and his angel wings grew . . . until the traumatic threes (that's my own spin). I remember when he turned three, we'd have chunks of time where he was so much fun and other times when I had no idea who stole my child and what was inhabiting his body. During these moments with our children, which happen throughout their development in different ways, I remember thinking, "How can I love someone this much and want to run away simultaneously?"

What I found the most challenging was the constant tantrums and his need to hang on me. The reservoir of patience I needed to summon to get through this was impressive. It required constant reminders that it is only temporary as he is melting down in the middle of a store and screaming or refusing to listen. I just witnessed a perfect example of this while sitting at the mall. A husband and wife were with their young daughter and son (the daughter looked about four and the son about two). As they were walking, their kids wanted to stop and look at the fountain, so they did that, but after a while, they decided to leave the fountain. Then all hell broke loose. Both kids started to melt down (mind you, it was lunchtime and probably close to nap time). As one parent picked up a child, the other parent went to grab the other one, and he dropped down like a dead weight in the middle of the mall.

The mother looked incredibly defeated as her husband's face grew red with frustration. It devolved into her husband picking both children up with a football hold and carrying them away from the fountain.

Now, most of us can connect with this example as it is extremely common. My mother always said it is cyclical, and they are six months in and six months out of bounds. This makes a lot of sense and is a good thing to hold onto. Knowing that the challenging moments of behavior will end is priceless in your quest to raise a healthy and well-rounded child. When you feel energetically drained or irritable, utilize your support system and "tap out." This is the best technique you can practice because you are of no use to anyone if you're angry and not thinking clearly. Utilizing our partners for support—or other loved ones if we are a single parent—is paramount to modeling what it means to take a pause or time-out for our children. Not only is it something we talk about, but it is also something we do to show them what healthy coping skills look like. That is magical and feels fantastic. You will only further your mommy guilt if you try to handle everything in the moment when you are tired, hungry, or angry, as you will not show up with grace. I have fallen from that pedestal a few times, and it hurts.

During this stage, attachment is crucial. You may have read or seen many things about attachment theory and various parenting styles. Ultimately, our goal as mothers is to create an environment where our children feel safe, protected, and nurtured. How we do that varies from mother to mother, but the essence remains the same. Consistency is critical in this stage (as with all stages) because our children learn to explore and know that we are there waiting for them when they return. Remaining consistent in our parenting creates that space of safety for our children while decreasing the angst of wondering if we will be there for them. Consistency is also crucial to our being; when we are inconsistent, tantrums can increase and take hold of us. We do ourselves a favor if we are consistent because we make our children aware of the boundaries. They can push until the cows come home, but we can and will stand firm in what we tell them. Now, don't beat yourself up if you waiver occasionally. We all have those moments where we don't have the fight in us, and that's okay. It's just about overall consistency. We also need to make sure we keep our anxiety in check as they explore. Our emotions radiate, and the first one it globs onto is our child. Watching our children learn to walk is exhilarating as we watch with pride. At the same time, we stand there holding our breath or run around next to them, moving anything that could potentially be hazardous to their new experience or themselves. You won't be able to protect them from every little thing, and this is where that lesson starts to sink in.

I know you're scared to do something wrong. It's normal. However, spending every day second-guessing yourself will take all the joy out of your parenting experience. Cuddle with your children when they are sad, love them no matter what, make repairs when you make mistakes, say you're sorry, and own your shit. Be the person who models the values you want them to embrace. Fear is real, and yet it will sabotage moments of fabulousness if you let it overrun your decisions. Regularly ask yourself in compassionate reflection, "Why am I making this decision?" Is it because that's what your parents did, or do you genuinely believe it's in your child's best interests? Get honest with yourself on a daily basis because the decisions you need to make as you age have more consequences that come along with them.

Speaking of the best interests of our children, I asked several women a question, and I am eager to share their responses.

Question to Moms: *How did becoming a mother impact your marriage/partnership?*

When posing this question, it was interesting to see how mothers responded. For the women in the thick of this stage, their responses often sounded something like this: "It's still a struggle on some days. It's so hard to build in date nights . . . being a mom often seems more important to me . . . but as my kids get older . . . I notice that it's just as important to show them good marriages and put time in for us parents. I also realize that parents need to be on the same page in front of the kids—kids notice more than we think. So, a strong, healthy marriage is important, and that means prioritizing the marriage. Easier said than done for many of us."

For those moms who were a little past this phase, they expressed how "I definitely had a challenging time parenting with my husband. He would give my children an emotional connection, and I felt left out and not connected to my husband. We needed to work on our relationship when my children were younger, and we attended counseling. We would fight a lot when the children were young. The children would split us, and we had a difficult time being on the same page. My husband and I were brought up differently, so that becomes challenging when making decisions regarding our children. Currently, we are doing the best that we have ever been, but it took work!"

Another said, "I'd often feel resentful being the primary caretaker, especially during the baby years when breastfeeding and being up all night. I realized my husband often had to be told what to do versus just knowing, which annoyed me. Now that my oldest of three kids is nine years old, we are finally getting into a good routine and know how to support each other, but it definitely takes constant effort."

For many mothers, having children can show you the tender parts of your marriage or the parts that need to be addressed. I have heard some mothers state: "It showed me the weaknesses in my relationship. It made the saying 'marriage takes work' the biggest understatement ever because having people depending on you and then realizing that you still have to make your spouse feel like they matter is a lot of work. And honestly, I didn't really want to put that energy into making him feel important anymore."

Another mom said, "I think it just made it more difficult because it feels impossible to ever be enough in all areas."

Here are some other responses that can offer insight into the impact of children on our marriages . . .

"It put a strain on my marriage due to not communicating some of the key things about raising a child beforehand. We were always at each other's throats, and so we didn't resolve the issues in a healthy way. I gave in, and it wasn't good; I should have fought behind the scenes to find a balance."

———

"The minute I had a child, nothing else mattered, and I neglected my husband. Being the best mother I could be was most important to me."

———

"I think it strengthened it because it was something we both wanted. My husband's job made his life extremely active, so he was gone a great deal as a police officer. Our roles were clearly defined, and we were both in agreement on them. He needed me to keep home life running smoothly, and I needed him to provide financially."

———

"In all ways—where do I begin? It's like asking if an alien landing in your backyard had an effect on your life."

From reviewing the above responses, it is evident our relationships are affected in a multitude of ways. Some of the biggest takeaways are the importance of staying connected regardless of how many children you have. Making time for your relationship is key, as well as being willing to work at connecting and reconnecting with your partner and knowing that this stage won't last forever. Don't take your partner for granted, and work together to get through this beautiful, challenging time in your lives; you will be better for it, and so will your children.

MOTHERHOOD DAILY CHECKLIST

1. What is one thing you are willing to let go of today so you can sit down to rest?
2. Take time to journal before bed.
3. Take a walk, even for only fifteen minutes. Just do it.
4. Connect with your partner if you haven't yet today by cuddling, watching something together, or talking.
5. How are you managing your stress level?

Action Step

How has being a mother impacted your marriage so far? If you don't have children yet, what are you learning you can do differently?

NOTES

_____
_____
_____
_____
_____
_____
_____
_____
_____
_____
_____
_____
_____
_____
_____
_____
_____
_____
_____
_____
_____
_____
_____
_____

CHAPTER 3

I'M JUST A MESS

Stage 3–Childhood

There are times when our children are growing up that we tend to feel lost. When life moves rapidly, it can seem as though we are just going through the motions. Over the years, I have connected with many mothers in this situation. They feel lost in their careers, at home with their families, or in life overall. This feeling can be all-consuming and quite scary at times. We may wake up and wonder, "What am I doing? Is this it? I don't know who I am right now." These thoughts are common during various transitions in our lives. Knowing that you are not alone is crucial. The next step is to take action to help you understand who you are at this particular juncture. Remember that the feelings of being adrift can be overwhelming and paralyzing. However, as uncomfortable as they may be, I believe that in these moments extraordinary growth can occur.

Food for Thought

When you are feeling lost, I challenge you to:

- Stop and observe your life. What do you see? What do you feel? What stands out to you?

- Next, write these things down so you can see them in black and white. Do you notice any patterns or themes? Do your feelings fill you up or bring you down?

- When considering the above, check in with yourself. How much time do you spend taking care of others versus taking care of yourself? Where do you fall on your priority list, and why? Many moms struggle with this because they feel they must care for everyone else first, leaving themselves last. The irony is that if you don't take care of yourself, you'll have nothing to give to others. You probably already know this, but it's true, and you need to make a change.

- Start identifying things you enjoy doing without your family. Yes, without them. When you spend all your time taking care of others and never have time alone, it can become confusing to distinguish their needs from your own. A little space is helpful and welcome; trust me, you'll enjoy it over time.

- Endeavor to do something just for you each week. Have your partner hold you accountable if necessary. If you already do this, increase the frequency to two or three times a week. The goal is to change your pattern and prioritize yourself.

- Take note of how you feel when you start taking better care of yourself and consider the message you're sending to your children. You're teaching them that it's okay to care for oneself and take time away to listen to our hearts and bodies when needed. Remember, children are influenced more by our actions than by our words.

- If the healthy choices you're making make you feel better, keep doing them!

- Understand that taking care of yourself doesn't mean neglecting your children's basic needs. It means finding a balance and ensuring their physical and emotional needs are met, whether by you or someone else, so you can step away briefly to rejuvenate.

Potty Training

Anticipating your child going to school can make the pressure of potty training unbearable. Whether your child goes to daycare or stays home with you, this milestone requires your participation in this momentous occasion. The end of diapers is a fabulous achievement! Regardless of whether you use the weekend no-diapers method or slowly introduce underwear, this process tests your patience and consistency. Let's be honest: it's helpful when daycare handles potty training during the day, giving you a bit of a reprieve. Remember, you can do it, and be patient with yourself. The only thing I ask is that you don't bribe your child with food. Food is for nourishment, not reward. Their reward should be your praise and excitement as they take on and conquer this new milestone.

School Transition

Now that you've navigated major hurdles like potty training, transitioning to a toddler bed, and starting daycare, you're ready for the next phase: school. It is at this juncture that our children are exposed to things we didn't realize were "a thing" until they start riding the school bus or talking with their friends. As your child's formal education begins, they will encounter new experiences, from riding the school bus to making friends. Initially, they may be excited about school, but as homework and extracurricular activities pile up, managing their exhaustion and enthusiasm becomes a balancing act.

During kindergarten through second grade, emotional breakdowns can become common. It's easy to worry about potential disorders, but often these behaviors are part of normal development. I promise you that while it may seem easier to diagnose our children with a disorder and have someone tell us how to fix it, more often than not, that's not the case. Yes, there are always exceptions, and I'm not saying there aren't genuine issues to address. However, jumping to a diagnosis as the first conclusion is often not the answer.

When your child's reactions seem disproportionately strong, remember that they often involve more than the immediate situation. They are navigating complex emotions, and our role is to stay calm, listen, and let them experience their feelings without judgment or punishment. Dig deep into your compassion reserves, especially during these challenging moments.

An important reminder: an emotionally dysregulated adult cannot regulate their child's emotions. If you can't manage your own emotions, teaching your child to manage theirs will be challenging. Children in school face overwhelming new experiences and emotions, and they need us to remain calm and supportive.

So . . . how can you teach your child something you don't know how to do for yourself? That's right, it's difficult. When our children start school, they experience the overwhelm of their peers, the structure of school, and the chaos of experiencing multiple emotions at the same time and having no idea what to do with them. As a result, it is essential for us to stay calm and on an even keel. Our children are going through a lot of different feelings, and, at the same time, it's hard to see they are struggling. They aren't *trying to be a nightmare*, even though it can feel that way. More often than not, our children are experiencing big emotions over things that in our mind seem out of proportion. *Seriously, you are crying and screaming because your crayon went out of the line while you were coloring?!*

We often, erroneously, come back with "how are you losing your shit statements" such as, "It's not a big deal!" or "Why are you crying over this?" (Hint: not helpful . . .)

The truth is, these statements are death in a situation like this, and I beg you to reconsider your stance. When our kids get to "that place," they need us to remain calm, listen, and let them experience these emotions without judging them or punishing them (interventions will definitely vary if they are harming themselves or another). Quite often, they need us to be curious without trying to fix it for them. When the reaction seems overblown for what you are witnessing, please remember it's not about the situation in front of you. There are almost always more emotions rising for them under the surface—you just aren't able to see them yet.

Now, with this knowledge in hand, I ask you to dig deep into your compassion reserves because these moments typically occur when you have very little left in your emotional cup. When your children are struggling, remember that they are not *trying* to make your life difficult; they are asking you to come closer. If you are able to rise to the task, you will feel much better.

During these times, it can be extremely overwhelming when we are coming home from a long day—whether it's taking care of our responsibilities at home or taking care of our responsibilities outside the home—and we may be exhausted. There are days when we feel like if one more thing is asked of us or goes awry, we may lose our shit and head for the hills. The reality is our children can feel that, and when we are short with them, it can start a downward spiral.

So what do we do?

FOOD FOR THOUGHT

- Gain deeper insight into how you manage your emotions. You can do this by reflecting on your upbringing. Think about when you felt different feelings: How did you handle them, and do you still handle them in the same way currently?

- Realize that your child doesn't understand that you had a bad day or are exhausted. They are at a stage where they see and feel your frustration as something they have done wrong—it's that simple. So it is imperative that you remember this when you walk through the door and potentially take your frustrations out on them—*you are their world*, and if you are unhappy, they immediately think it's because it's their fault, and they have made you unhappy.

- Parents need "time-outs" too. If you feel yourself becoming escalated and know you must step away, do it. Ask your partner to jump in. Take a time-out. Hop in the shower, or take a walk to reset and return. The best thing we can do is model the behavior we would like our children to embrace.

Asking for Help

As your children grow, you'll realize you need help and can't do everything alone. Accepting help from your partner, family, or friends is crucial. But avoid micromanaging their efforts. Trust them and be open to their valuable contributions. It's important to step outside your comfort zone and try different approaches. I know we, as moms, think we know best. To be fair, our partners and loved ones may have some really valuable contributions to parenting but we, at times, can let our own judgment, fear, and apprehension get in the way. Sometimes, it's really easy to lose sight of the fact that none of us do or will do this perfectly, so we need to stop with the delusion that our way is the only way.

My work with Carla is a perfect example of this. We started working together because she was enraged that her partner didn't do enough to help with the kids. She would repeatedly express that he only cares about himself, does whatever he wants, and isn't around to help when she needs support. As we looked a little deeper, we discussed the way they engaged in a particular pattern. She would begin by asking him to pack a bag for an outing with the children. Her partner would happily pack the bag only to be informed later on that he did it wrong—as he forgot their child's snacks. Is neglecting to bring snacks going to make or break the outing? Likely not. But this exchange makes her partner feel as though his help is not appreciated. When criticized, it becomes more difficult for him to volunteer to help when he is accused of doing everything wrong, over and over again, under differing circumstances.

Holding ourselves accountable for our emotions allows us to be brave enough to step outside of our comfort zones and try something different. If we don't, we will feel empty and lost for longer periods of time because we are not actively helping ourselves.

Think about the people in your life that you can ask for help. Explore what help you are comfortable with them providing; for some people, it may be taking your kids for a few hours. For others, maybe it's an occasional overnight visit. The truth is, it's important that you have separation from your children—whether for their sake or yours—it's absolutely necessary. It's also healthy to start instituting small increments of separation when they are little. Have that date night you dreamed about—or just get your nails done. How can we expect our kids to step outside their comfort zone when they are nervous if we won't?

Partner Collaboration

Collaborating with your partner on parenting strategies can be challenging. Different views on discipline, for example, require open communication and compromise. Discuss your family values early on, understand each other's approaches, and find a middle ground.

It can feel uncomfortable to work together with our partner on ways in which we think we should address our child's behaviors. This can be a dicey topic in many households. To be honest, this can be where single parents think, "Thank God I call all the shots with no one else's opinion." One parent may think discipline looks like having a conversation, while the other parent feels a consequence should be implemented. Navigating this terrain can have its pitfalls, to say the least. I have found that it's essential to remember there is no perfect way and you are regularly walking the fine line of parenting together—or alienating each other—if you're not coming up with a solution you can both get behind. My mother always says, "You need to make it a win-win," and boy, is she right.

The key to these discussions is to have them in private—away from your children—and to be open to hearing how another approach could be beneficial. For example, if your son is acting out and throwing a tantrum, possibly even screaming and punching you, maybe you would like to give him a time-out while your partner wants to impose a consequence of taking away his favorite truck. Oftentimes, when these situations arise, we don't know how we are going to handle them and the fear of doing it wrong can creep in. I suggest having some of these conversations early on in your child-rearing, just to gauge how close—or far apart—you are on these topics. For some situations, you won't know until you are in it, and in that case, having the conversation after the situation is key. Be open to hearing why your partner feels their way is beneficial, and then ask each other, *Where do you see the compromise?* This may look like you are putting your son in time-out one or two times, and if that doesn't work, implementing a consequence. This way, you are honoring both of your approaches . . . You get the point.

A great exercise early on in your child-rearing is for you and your partner to sit down separately and write a list of your family values. After you have each written your list of values, next to them, I want you to write how you exhibit those values in your behavior. Then, I want you both to come together and share your lists with each other and see where they are in alignment and where they are not. Hold yourselves accountable to make sure your behavior is congruent with your values. This will allow you to have an outline from which your parenting will evolve and keep you grounded in what you want to teach your children.

- **Discuss and Align Values:** Write down your family values and how you exhibit them. Share these with your partner to align your parenting approach.
- **Handle Discipline Together:** Agree on how to handle discipline, balancing both approaches. For instance, use time-outs first and then consequences if needed.

Gratitude and Patience

You may feel like you've repeated yourself a thousand times during this stage. Yes, you may get tired of hearing yourself talk while also wishing your name wasn't "mom." I remember the days when my son would say "mom" what felt like a million times within a few hours, and I fantasized that I would change my name or put in earplugs so I couldn't hear it anymore. It's normal to get tired of hearing your own voice and wish for a break. These are the moments to lean on the support system you've built. It is also in these times that we learn the art of gratitude that we can have children at all—so try to cherish the journey, even on the tough days.

MOTHERHOOD DAILY CHECKLIST

Ask Yourself:

1. "Have I tried stepping outside my comfort zone?"
2. "Am I meeting my own needs?"
3. "What fills my emotional bucket? Have I done that recently?"
4. "Do I feel balanced? If not, why? Am I managing my emotions in a healthy way so I am modeling what emotion regulation can look like for my children?"

Question to Moms: *What have you learned about being a mom that you want other moms to know?*

"It truly takes a village to raise a child . . . It's good to have a village, so talk to others and let others help you."

———

"I have learned a lot about being patient, learning when they were young that I followed their sleep schedule. I noticed that other mothers compared me to them a lot of the time. My kids were different from other kids. What worked for me didn't work for other mothers or children. I also noticed how much my body changed after giving birth. It was a difficult period to schedule time for exercise, and time with my husband was difficult as well. When he wanted attention, I was exhausted. Making space to have alone time together on date night was important for us to connect and be on the same page. Parenting changed our relationship—we had our ups and downs."

———

"It's an indescribable love that is the best feeling in the world, but at the same time the most challenging job in the world."

———

"That it's wonderful and I love it."

———

"Be prepared for your entire life to change; every aspect of your life will change, so be prepared to be sad, worried, tired, and the happiest you could imagine a lot and all at the same time."

———

"That it's nothing like you expect it to be—and so much more. It forces you to be present."

———

"Never do it—[said jokingly]. Seriously, these are my tips:

Make sure you and your spouse are on the same page about education and discipline prior to having children; otherwise, your child runs back and forth and splits.

The internet causes anxiety—keep them off as much as possible.

Give them limits and make sure they rest."

————

"You'll never love anything like you love your kids and you don't need to be married for a second opinion—in my house, our division of labor was I parented, and my husband financially supported us."

————

"I want people to know that you can never give up as a mom. No matter what stage of motherhood you're in. It's not an easy feat and you need to prepare yourself for that."

————

"When you reach my age, you look at things a lot differently because you realize that things that were important then really aren't that important. You can never go wrong by loving your children and letting them know. I thought if I did ABC that DEF would be the outcome—that is not the case because your children are all different individuals with different personalities and different issues. 2 + 2 doesn't always equal 4."

————

"I have learned that being a mom is one of the most challenging jobs a woman can have. The responsibility of grooming a child for this world can be frightening."

————

"I learned that it is essential to give unconditional love. Give them room to grow into who they are intended to be. Listen to them and take an interest in what interests them. And that no matter how things appear, the direction of their life is not set; realize that some take longer than others to blossom."

Action Step

What are you learning about yourself now that you have a child/children?

Notes

61

_____
_____
_____
_____
_____
_____
_____
_____
_____
_____
_____
_____
_____
_____
_____
_____
_____
_____
_____
_____
_____
_____
_____
_____
_____
_____
_____
_____

CHAPTER 4

I LOVE THIS FREEDOM, BUT . . .

Stage 4–Late Childhood into Early Adolescence

It's incredible how each stage of our children's growth brings significant changes. As they change, we need to adapt and grow with them, adjusting our approaches and trying new strategies. The freedom you feel when your children start dressing themselves and following routines is wonderful. It feels like a weight has been lifted, as they no longer rely on you for every single need (though being a mom never truly ends, of course, but it is joyous when they can get their own snack). Remember, we play a large role in our own freedom. What I mean is that if we keep our children dependent on us out of fear of them becoming age-appropriately independent, we are creating our own lack of freedom. We avoid the discomfort of letting go, but this issue becomes more crucial as they grow older. We face it at each stage of their development, and it's essential to address it to foster their independence. A great friend of mine said, "Parenting comes with a lot of grieving at each stage." When we spoke further, she expressed that each milestone marks the end of what once was and the beginning of what is unknown. So my question to all mothers reading this is: How are you dealing with your grieving? Are you allowing yourself to feel the sadness around what you miss about your child's younger years? Or do you find yourself hanging with other moms, drinking wine while your kids play, and talking about how hard life is?

My client Judy and I would talk about how she found herself drinking more and more recently but was unaware as to why she was, as she hated alcohol. She expressed feeling like her children are growing up and don't need her as much anymore, which scares her, and she wasn't sure of her role in their lives. She felt confident in her ability as a mom to meet their physical needs, but as her children got older and needed more of her emotional energy, she felt out of her comfort zone. Therefore, she tried to manage that feeling by numbing it with alcohol. Feeling the sadness and grief was overwhelming to Judy, so we worked on feeling it in small, more tolerable increments so she could gain trust in her ability to manage these emotions instead of running from them. I want to encourage you to *feel the sadness*, embrace the emotion, and take those trips down memory lane on your photo reel when you need to. Allow yourself that time and space to remember those precious moments at each stage of their development. It's healthy to do so, in order for you to grow, but it's just as imperative that you don't stay stuck there. There's no going back! As moms, we are tasked with making sure we allow space for our children to develop into who they are meant to be— not who we want them to become. So ask yourself, am I allowing my child to express their true self?

As mothers, we are going through consecutive rebirths along this parenting journey, so we need to check in with ourselves and ask if we are doing so authentically. There is no right or wrong way, but there are definitely little things we learn that are extremely helpful to our growth that allow us to support that of our child's. As I have referenced in *The Gut Check: How to Reconnect with Your Intuition*, letting go is not always as easy as people declare it to be. In the process of letting go, we need to make sure we are honoring what needs to be released, why we need to let it go, and what the benefits will be once we are able to. Some of this change requires a leap of faith in order for us to step into the unknown with grace and a sense of calm, knowing that no matter what happens, we are ready for what's to come.

Letting go at this stage involves addressing your own anxieties and fears (yes, yet again) that come up when your child wants to go play in the yard with a friend without you sitting outside watching their every move. Or perhaps your child wants to venture up to the neighbor's house without you holding their hand. These are some minor examples of instances that you will be presented with, and you will have choices to make. Now, as we know, it's not always black and white. We need to assess our child's ma-turity at different ages and have clarity around the trust that has—or has not—been built for them to take these next steps. We also need to get real with the fact that they are going to make mistakes—and that doesn't always mean there should be consequences. It will depend on the behavior.

This is a perfect example of the nuances that we, as moms, balance on any given day to assess whether we are making a healthy decision. Couple this with multiple chil-dren who have varying personalities, and you now have a perfect storm of confusion and indecision. But I promise you—you *will* figure it out . . .

Speaking of letting go, let's talk about how hard it is to watch our children begin to experience peer pressure and navigate these relationships. Seeing our children sad or heartbroken over relationship issues, as they are trying to develop their friend groups or start wanting a partner when they hit middle school, can feel like a slow form of torture. The best advice I can give all moms is to work on your listening skills. We walk that fine line judiciously, carefully supporting our children—but not saying too much— loving them but not smothering them, and helping them develop healthy coping skills while making sure they don't rely on everyone else. This is a delicate balance that we face on a daily basis. When we say too much, we tend to shut our children down—and then they talk less. At this juncture, the key to a healthy relationship with our children is to allow them to feel heard and to hone our ability to keep our mouth shut. I know this may be a shocker, but we don't know everything—nor do we have all the answers—so why do we need to pretend like we do? It makes no sense. Do we want to pass down falsities or untruths to them? I'd prefer not to.

When our children come to us with relationship concerns, very often, we experience their pain as our own. It is typically this discomfort of pain, sadness, or hurt that we struggle to sit with on our own, so how are we going to support our children through theirs? We need to deal with our emotional baggage, because if we don't, it will bleed into our ability to parent our children in a healthy way, and we will inadvertently pass along the things that do not serve them well. Take some time to think about what emotions are most challenging for you to sit with and why. What do you need when you feel pain? More often than not, we are looking for comfort and nurturing in those times in some way, shape, or form. Now, we know each child deals with things differently, so when they are struggling, don't ever be afraid to ask your child, "What do you need?" You may be surprised by their insight into themselves. You don't have to have all the answers, but you need to allow the discomfort of tough feelings to fill the room once in a while. The better we manage our own emotions, the more helpful we can be at helping our children to manage theirs.

It's interesting to note that what we can fail to understand at this stage when their peer relationships are changing is that it may change our relationships with their friends' parents. Some mothers become friends with their child's friends' parents, while other mothers choose to keep them at a distance. What no one prepares you for, regardless of how close you are to your child's friend's mother when the kids have issues, is that different emotions manifest differently in each mother. This can be hairy to navigate. Every mom has a singular emotional tolerance for their child's pain. While some mothers are okay with their child working through these peer issues independently, other moms are not. You will learn a lot about your friends, and it's essential to be willing to reevaluate these friendships if need be.

That said, how do you deal with your emotions around all the different logistics that take place at this stage in your life? Managing the logistics of extracurricular activities, band, dance, dinner, bedtime routine . . . the list goes on. It can be exhausting at best, whether you have one child or several. Add this to having a relationship, a job (regardless of whether it's in or out of the home), caring for parents, and you have entered a chaotic time that becomes the new normal. There are many days where it feels like your head is spinning—and it just may spin completely off if you don't take a time-out for yourself. Moms tend to be the keeper of all things logistical—yes, there are exceptions to every rule, and this isn't a hard and fast one, just more of an observation. With this duty comes a lot of pressure to have a good memory and an airtight time management system in place. All too often, we can be guilty of allowing our first child to get involved in all the activities they want and realize when they get older or another child comes along that we may have overcommitted. And now it feels like there's no turning back. Take a deep breath . . . we can always pivot. Often, we confine ourselves, feeling like we can't change anything, that we are stuck, or there's no way out. The reality is there is always a way out; we just have to take some time in solitude to get clarity on what that is.

I know, you're saying, "How the hell am I going to take time in solitude with all this madness going on? I can't even go to the bathroom without someone banging on the door or yelling my name." Well, not to be harsh, but it's on you. If you want something to change, you need to change it, and if you don't know how, reach out for help. Our partners can often see things about us that we may or may not want to see in ourselves, but this is a gift. The gift is a change in perspective. Now, say you choose to access this gift—what will you do with it once you have it? It's so easy to get mad at our partners when we feel like we are doing everything, but the reality is our families will allow us to do as much as we continue to do because there is a benefit; they are receiving it!

If we feel like we are doing too much and can't take one more thing, that's on us to change and no one else. When you realize you have overcommitted, stop and look at what support you need and how you can be receptive to it. I hear so many women express that they are exhausted and burned out, yet they are not willing to relinquish any control or power over to their partner. At that point, you can't be mad at your partner if they have expressed a willingness to help but you won't let them, as we have discussed in earlier stages.

In mentioning difficult conversations (you know, the one where you ask for help . . . ?), you can plan to have many more in the future. In this stage, as your child or children continue to grow emotionally and start putting different pieces together about themselves and the world around them, these sorts of conversations can be extremely insightful and exhilarating. But hey . . . I am a therapist. What I have experienced is the beauty of my boys feeling comfortable asking some tough questions and making some really impressive observations. What I love about this stage is their curiosity and openness to understanding what they are learning. That could be the gift of riding the school bus or "the sex talk" that starts in sixth-grade health. Either way, if we take the time to listen, we give our kids a fantastic gift.

Now, the difficulty that comes along with listening to their day, in school or on the bus, is being able to hold our tongue when something happens that triggers us in some way. It is so important to be cognizant of our reaction so we don't deter them from future communications. It's crucial to understand how these difficult conversations make us feel. Sometimes, the conversations are scary, sometimes angst-producing, and other times, they are brimming with pride. Regardless of the emotion, it is important that we allow ourselves the time and space to process those emotions at a different point to ensure we are not passing on any generational trauma.

A specific, complex conversation that can arise at this time is one around gender or sexuality. Late childhood and early adolescence seems to be a common time for children to start questioning themselves, their likes, and their place in the world as their hormones start to take hold. Being willing to listen to their feelings, fears, and desires without judgment may be taxing—but it is also one of the most rewarding things you can do. Here is where some moms struggle with grief, yet again, while others can embrace the path their child is taking. You can be the most well-rounded and healthy mother in the world and still have an emotional reaction to your child informing you of a change in their gender or sexuality. This can trigger a myriad of emotions depending on our belief systems, upbringing, and the vision we have for our child. It is entirely natural and okay to have mixed feelings when being given some intense information. I encourage you to take time to process; just listen and talk when you are able to respond thoughtfully—not react. I honor that you are trying to balance these moments by making sure your child feels seen and accepted while trying to navigate how you feel about the information you are processing in that moment. It's a lot to take in, and taking your time to unpack it is okay.

For me, this age and onward is my sweet spot. While some moms do well with infants, I do well with preteens and teenagers. Don't get me wrong, it can be highly demanding, but I really enjoy the challenges it presents. What I have found is that when we feel confident in our ability to handle whatever comes our way, our children pick up on this energy and feel more comfortable sharing the nitty-gritty. From sex to cursing, this time frame keeps us on our toes. I strongly encourage moms to think about what conversations make you uncomfortable and why. The earlier in your motherhood you are able to ask yourself these hard questions, the more apt you will be to face the discomfort head-on, with your children. In my eyes, this is a priceless skill that everyone should learn. It's okay to feel a little out of your comfort zone with this age. Don't beat yourself up for feeling unsure how to handle certain situations; it's normal. But when you notice those times have crept up on you, take the time and space you need to process them so you can give your child a healthy response instead of a reaction. Very rarely will you feel bad about taking time to embrace the awareness of your emotional state as it will only benefit you and your family in the long run.

The other love I share for this stage of motherhood is that I don't feel like I have to be with my children all the time, as they are learning to explore and spend time alone to sit with themselves when they aren't attached to their devices. Even in loving this stage, there can still be some apprehension around how much freedom to allow them and how to slowly back off. That is a balance that I feel is child-specific. This is where it can be tricky navigating with your partner as you may have different levels of distress tolerance. What I mean by that is you may feel comfortable managing your angst of letting your son ride his bike around the neighborhood without you present. In contrast, your partner may not feel this is age-appropriate, and it makes them extremely nervous. This is the beginning of some interesting discussions trying to figure out where your comfort level lies and what's the most age-appropriate approach to give them some autonomy— but not too much. These moments can also create fear as a result of feeling like you have diminishing influence over your child and their values. What I want to assure you of is that you still have a great deal of influence, no matter how it feels. I want to encourage you to stay strong in your values, whether you feel your children are listening or not, and do not get discouraged . . . They will hear you someday, and they are watching you every day.

As a society, I feel we have been confronted by the realization that if we don't get over our own fears or anxieties, we are essentially sending the message to our children that we don't trust they can handle things. It follows, then, that we aren't giving them space to build confidence in the choices they make without us present. Truth be told, we need to handle our emotions so our children can grow into healthy young adults without our "stuff" getting in the way.

Another way in which we send a message of not trusting is to our partners. It has been shown repeatedly when I meet with mothers that they feel as though they need to be the "go between" or "mediator" between their children and their fathers. I think we need to stop and ask ourselves, *Why is this?* For many, it's because we feel our approach to handling situations is much better (funny and true, all at the same time), while in other instances, it is fear of how our children will internalize our partner's approach. Either way, we need to learn how to step back. When we continue to insert ourselves, we are not allowing our partner to feel as though their parenting holds as much significance as our own. We are also depriving ourselves of the emotional release from not having to handle more than we already have on our plates. That sounds quite fabulous, doesn't it?

When your child or partner comes to you about a situation they had with each other, it's okay to listen and then refer them back to each other. Give them the space to develop their own relationship and determine what they want that to look like. This will also help you develop the trust that when you need your self-care days, you can do so and not have to worry what "shit show" you may be walking back into.

I have also found that trust is essential when giving our children some freedom. It feels scary and requires us to lean on friends and other moms that we value and respect to help us get through the worry that surfaces. A perfect example is when my son wanted to start walking around the mall on his own, with a friend or his girlfriend. Now, I am all about encouraging freedom, and yet I was also nervous to take this step with all the fears about, "What if someone snatches him up? What if he gets hurt? What if . . . what if . . . ?" These fears are natural and healthy, alerting us to be cautious. But we also have to invite ourselves to face the fear. In this one specific situation where he wanted to walk the mall with his girlfriend, I spoke with her mother, and we came up with a plan together that felt good—but nudged us both to step outside our comfort zones to give them a chance to show they are ready for this next step. I stayed in the mall the whole time while giving them space and we agreed they would come to check in with me at specific times.

The other internal struggle we often face as moms is how to decipher what age-appropriate steps are. You can read all the parenting books in the world, and yet some things may feel like a huge stretch for your child at a certain age, and other things seem trivial. This is where I want to remind you it's truly about you tuning into your gut instinct and determining what emotions are at play—fear, discomfort, hesitation—and which emotion is guiding your decision-making at that time. Being able to distinguish between your "mommy intuition" and your fear is going to be key to making the healthiest decisions possible.

FOOD FOR THOUGHT

- Let go . . .

- Listen . . .

- What emotions of your own do you struggle to sit with and why?

- Be willing to pivot when things aren't working.

- What conversations make you uncomfortable, and why?

- Be willing to lean into the discomfort.

- Respond, don't react.

MOTHERHOOD DAILY CHECKLIST

1. Am I being adaptable?
2. What am I grieving, and how am I managing it?
3. What do I need to let go of?
4. Am I letting my child build trust even though it makes me nervous?
5. Am I being a good listener for myself and others?

Question to Moms: *What was the most challenging stage of motherhood for you and why?*

"With my firstborn, it was the very beginning . . . but as I became more seasoned with child number 2 and number 3, I began to love the beginning. I needed to learn to soak up the quiet moments when they sleep all day and not rush the growth."

———

"I found it the most challenging when my children would talk back to me, have a tantrum in public, didn't accept 'no' for an answer. I also found it difficult when they didn't eat the food I prepared and would throw their food when they were a toddler/preschooler. Additionally, I found it difficult when my children would listen to their father more than they would listen to me, and then we would be in a big argument the rest of the night. I found my husband would give in to them more than I would, and then I would be the 'mean parent.'"

———

"The infant years when juggling multiple kids and trying to find the right balance between kids, my husband, work, extended family, friends, and my individual interests, which seemed nonexistent."

———

"The first month because it's a life change—now you have to take care of someone else and be sleep deprived."

———

"Baby/newborn—being homebound, feeling trapped, secluded, alone, and scared. It was all so unknown, and I didn't have a ton of support. I was super anxious to leave my house and I got into a place of being a hermit and secluding myself."

———

"Learning how to manage being a full-time working mother because you never feel like you're giving enough time to your child. There's a lot of guilt for leaving them."

———

"They were all great years until she started junior high, around age twelve—when our daughter started acting out and my husband and I weren't on the same page regarding how to discipline her. Because we weren't on the same page, she was splitting us and then everyone in the house was fighting—myself and my daughter and myself and my husband."

———

"When I realized my son, in second grade, had learning disabilities and health impairments. It was difficult because I had to watch my child struggle with everyday things—such as getting picked on."

———

"The teenage years were the most challenging (ages twelve to fifteen) because that's when your children want to explore, and they tend to follow their friends. Your children want to make more decisions for themselves at this time and they aren't necessarily able to."

————

"When they were little, it was fun, and they did as I wanted them to. It's challenging as your children want to make decisions, but they aren't always in their best interests or appropriate and they struggle with their parents' rules."

————

"Even though it's the most challenging, it was the most rewarding as you see your children form the foundation and basis of becoming an adult as they question the process and form their own opinions. I think this is the most important time in their lives when they need to know they are an important part of a family unit."

————

"The most difficult stage of motherhood for me is the stage I'm in right now. My son has issues that prevent him from 'launching,' and I must garner as much patience as possible to deal with his issues currently."

————

"It was difficult being a mother to teenagers. They were going through their own physical and mental turmoil from just being a teenager, and no matter how loving I was to them, I was the enemy that nagged."

"The most difficult stage of motherhood was a result of coming to the realization that one of my children was an addict. I had to come to a place of surrender, a letting go, by accepting the fact that I was powerless to rescue him. As a mother, care of my children took a high priority, but that care had to become totally hands-off."

Action Step

What has been (or do you anticipate being in the future) the most difficult stage of parenting for you and why?

NOTES

CHAPTER 5

I'M NOT READY FOR THEM TO GO TO COLLEGE!

Stage 5–Adolescence into Young Adulthood

When our children are little, we may not realize that, as they grow older, our connection—and our boundaries with them —also evolve. Navigating these changes can create uncertainty. Are we walking the line "appropriately"? Adaptability is a key element of our sanity as a mom. At times, I've found it challenging to determine how much to share with them. I struggle to determine what I should share about the world as I have experienced it, and how to allow them to experience it independently without my bias. We often feel an intense urge to warn, protect, and prepare, and yet there are times when you truly can't prepare someone for an experience. They need to have the experience on their own terms, in their own time, in order to grow. Keeping my mouth shut can be extremely challenging when all I want to say is, "What the hell are you thinking?!" I find myself using self-talk to let the situation play out. I feel it's essential to allow our reaction internally, or to discuss it with our partner, to plan the best approach in addressing certain situations. This way, we know we are dealing with it in line with our values and supporting our children's growth.

Of course, there are times when things fly out of my mouth. And I do apologize to my children if it was rough or reactionary. I consciously attempt to minimize those events, but admittedly, they occur. It's also easy for us to be fooled by our child's apparent maturity and that they can handle it if we share certain things about our lives. However, I'd like to remind you they may not be ready for those discussions until they are much older. Balancing your truths with their maturity can be tricky; using discernment is paramount.

Being mindful of our children's maturity also informs how we appropriately prepare them for young adulthood while still meeting their need for protection and nurturing. I know this is a ubiquitous question for all mothers. Once again, what we experience is a process of questioning. *How do I help them manage all these different aspects of getting older?*

If you think about it, we want to help our children feel confident and minimize their anxiety. Yet, the only way they will learn how to manage it is by experiencing things and attempting to find various ways to cope with challenging situations. The message is, don't allow your inability to manage your fears to get in the way of enabling them to manage theirs. Take time to reassess your values with your partner and evaluate whether your behaviors are congruent with your values as a person, and the values you hope to instill in your children.

The beauty is that we are looking honestly at what we have taught them over the years. We need to trust that all we have given them and the values we have instilled will be taken on as their own. This may be difficult when our children feel comfortable enough to give us feedback about how *they* feel we have been, as a mom. Yes, this can occur, and it can be amazing and thorny, all at the same time. I want to remind you, when your children give you feedback about your parenting, just listen. They are testing the boundaries, speaking their truth, and seeking validation from us for some growth process to happen. When we see our children taking on some of our values while at the same time discovering some of their own ideals, I want you to know that it doesn't mean you have done a poor job. Sometimes, we need to stray a little to find ourselves and see what fits and what doesn't. Growth isn't linear. As moms, we know this firsthand. Once more, I want to encourage all moms not to take their child's decisions or path in life so personally. Easier said than done, but incredibly necessary to get through motherhood.

There is no right or wrong way to get through these issues, and with each child we raise, the landscape looks different. We will have some children who want to leave as soon as they graduate and some who, if we let them, would stay home forever. We will have some children who struggle with neurodiversity, and their launch into the world looks different. They may require more support from us than a child with a different makeup. Regardless of which child you have, make sure you check in with yourself about what is best and most supportive in the launch phase. Sometimes, setting your expectations aside for where you thought they should be is required so you can meet them where they are. Doing so allows space for their confidence in this transition to flourish by showing them there is no shame in being right where they are at this particular juncture. Now . . . if we all could take that advice and use it with ourselves, the world would be an easier place to navigate, wouldn't it? Balancing our needs and relationships as we try to teach our children how to balance theirs can be problematic.

On one hand, as parents, we consistently put our needs aside. On the other hand, we don't realize how many of our own needs or issues sneak in when we aren't looking. Potentially, this can be one of the greatest barriers at this stage in our journey as mothers.

In our desire to be a good mom and meet the needs of our children and spouses, our relationships with the ones we love outside of our immediate family go through many ebbs and flows, as all relationships do, but for very different reasons. When our children are little, we have playdates with our friends and their kids. Then, as our children get older and become involved in their chosen activities, our time becomes more restricted. Our investment in external relationships takes more of a back seat as we are pulled in many directions. Then, once our children reach high school and college age, we realize we have more freedoms, which can sometimes feel strangely foreign. Our minds race, thinking, "What will I do with my time?" "Maybe I need to join a club . . ." "I don't have any friends." And the list goes on. How you manage your time and energy along the journey of mothering will play a role in how these changes impact you at each stage.

I often hear moms say, "I don't have time," or "Where am I supposed to find time for that?" My response is to *make time*. This requires us to say "no" to some things and "yes" to others. We determine how our time is spent each day that we live. We decide what we agree to and what we refuse to do. If you don't feel you have enough time where you want to spend it, change it before you regret the time you lost.

When working with my client Janet, she would come into each session and say, "I don't have time for anything . . ."

We regularly explored how she felt like her life was passing her by as she was running from one event to the next. Life was becoming untenable between working, being a wife, and a mother. In one session, I asked her to make a pie chart of where her time is spent and then to write the percentage of time allotted to each category of her life in each "piece." Once she saw this, she was able to determine how to split the pie a little differently. I asked her to make a new pie chart that accurately reflected how she *wanted* to spend her time. We then compared the two. Finally, I asked Janet to write down what changes she could make to start the shift from pie one to pie two, no matter how big or small the actions were. This was a crucial step as I wanted her to have them on paper to reference as she progressed.

I want to encourage all of you to refer back to the skills discussed in earlier chapters—and ask for help. You are not a "lone ranger" who is charged with all the responsibilities for the entire family. Find a way to keep yourself connected to things and people who fulfill you—to the extent that feels right for you. Some mothers need an extensive network of friends, while others prefer a small circle. Know yourself and get your "queen time" in because once your children start to show up in the world on their own, you will want these supports in place.

Our friendships and relationships with our siblings and parents can also be extremely grounding, especially during stress or transition. Reminder . . . it takes a village, so "return to the village" when you need a reprieve; you can always borrow their strength.

In these times of transition, we need to be willing to reassess our approach and our assumptions, regularly. Stepping back to evaluate if we are allowing our maladaptive thoughts to interfere with our ability to be present for our growing children can be intense on a good day. Being able to see that, even though we think something should happen a certain way, or in our experience, it worked best "this way," doesn't necessarily mean it will work in the same way for our children. Take time to think about what your child is doing that triggers you or brings up intense feelings. Asking yourself these types of questions can be quite informative.

And it doesn't stop there; we also need to be able to transform this information into actionable steps. In other words, we need to be flexible and adaptable. I have found it exhausting at times. I want to ask everyone, "Can't one thing work for more than two minutes, please?" The moments when we feel like we constantly need to course-correct, or try a different approach, or speak differently to our children, can be extremely taxing. It can make us feel like we are walking on eggshells. We may feel insecure as we put pressure on ourselves to *instinctively* know how to help and heal our family. Reminder . . . you're not an oracle as much as you may feel you need to be at times. When you get to that spot where you feel like you are doing the "fire walk" because you are worried about choices your child is making, and they get frustrated when you voice your opinion, it's time to check in with yourself and see what is really bothering you.

The "fire walk" is why moms often struggle with the thought of children going away to college or moving out of the house. In part, it triggers a feeling of "Wait, they are going to leave . . . ?" For others, it generates apprehension about what their purpose will be once their child flies the nest. Some parents fear losing that connection or are unsure how their connection will change. This uncertainty can make us hold on tighter—even smother them—which typically doesn't end well. They are searching for more freedom, and our fear is that they don't need (or want) us to be around any longer. The fear is real, the feeling is strong, and I assure you, the love will remain. I encourage you to confront your worries and allow them space while reeling them back in when needed. Be open with your emotions. Tell your children you miss them and want to remain connected. Set intentional time aside to do things together. In these times, we are faced with the push/pull. It is a time when we are wistful about missing the last stages of parenting and being excited for what's to come. As all of these stages unfold, we also become privy to the fact that we may not have maintained some of the other relationships in our lives.

The need to handle our emotions will never end. And they can certainly be triggered, mainly when our children are in high school and the conversation regarding college looms large. These discussions can be overwhelming on so many levels that we must handle them in smaller increments. Over the course of a few sessions, my client Maggie and I talked at length about how her daughter had hopes of going to a college that costs a small fortune. However, Maggie and her husband couldn't afford it. Not only was the price tag steep, but they also weren't sure if their daughter would have the grades to get accepted—but she was convinced she had a sure shot. When Maggie's daughter first approached her about applying, Maggie understandably had a knee-jerk reaction. She replied somewhat sarcastically, "You're not serious, are you?" Her daughter was astonished. "Of course I am serious! What . . . you don't think I can get accepted?" As you can imagine, this conversation took a sharp turn into "Dumpsville" very quickly, and it wasn't pretty. In her daughter's reply, Maggie realized her initial reaction probably wasn't the most thoughtful. She also realized that her response to her daughter's reaction needed to be delicate and loving. It was at that moment that Maggie could authentically step into all the work she had accomplished in therapy, taking a pause and responding instead of reacting. As she thoughtfully replied to her daughter, the conversation went very well, and they were both able to re-center. This set the tone for many healthy discussions in the future.

Okay . . . let's talk more about money. If you haven't started looking at the cost of college, I will give you a heads-up—it can be steep. Everyone has a different experience of the hunt for college based on financial background, level of education, and money management prior to having children. Regardless of your socioeconomic status, the transition to college and confronting the reality of your finances as they relate to your child's education can be daunting. Time and time again, I see families striving to support their children financially in an effort to ease the financial burden for them—often at the cost of their retirement plans. Some even refinance their homes while not holding their child accountable for having some financial skin in the game. As a result, many difficulties can come your way if you aren't thinking it through beforehand. Some of the problems we encounter include the inability to retire because the money we had set aside is no longer there. Sadly—and of course this doesn't happen with all children—there are also times that they do not take their education seriously enough because they mistakenly think that the "money tree" is on a never-ending growth spurt. Many of them are also unaware—and unaffected—by all the hoops we hop through behind the scenes to help them. Finally, I have seen some children show very little gratitude for their parents' financial sacrifices. Painfully, this can show up as resentment from their parents, fracturing the relationship.

Employ this knowledge when discussing college with your spouse ahead of time. Get clear on what you are—and are not—willing to do and stick to a plan. Ensure you have these conversations with your children in high school so you can patiently manage your emotions and their expectations.

And it's not just about college. Money is undoubtedly one of the main aspects of growing into young adulthood. As we are trying to support our children in emotion regulation, the same concept applies to finances. I will give you an example. In our family, financial literacy is critical. I feel strongly about teaching children how to make, save, and manage money. The way I see it is that the earlier you start this process through open, age-appropriate discussion, the better. Navigating this can be tricky. What should a parent pay for, and what should be considered luxuries? I have conceptualized it in my head in this way: the necessities are always covered (things such as food, clothing, and shoes), and if they want specialty items outside of what is deemed a necessity, then they can use their money to purchase them. This can be a tricky line to walk, and there may be exceptions here and there—but that's okay. Many of these decisions require a little contemplation. Get quiet with yourself and take the time to *feel*. That's right, I said the naughty "f" word. Feeling is essential so you sense, in your gut, that it's the right choice. If you don't get that feeling, pause before you decide. Simply because our children want a decision *now* doesn't mean we must give it to them.

When our children graduate from high school and go to college, it can be extremely sad due to the bond we create with them. Conversely, it can be a relief to some who struggle to live in the same home with their child as they come into their own as a young adult. I want to assure you that there is no good reason to feel bad if you are relieved about your child going away to school. It doesn't make you a bad mom. I encourage you to look at it from the perspective of "my child is becoming their own person and learning how they like to do things, which can be different from us." It's beautiful that they feel safe enough to express themselves and assert their autonomy. However, it can also be frustrating as you try to navigate giving them this space to voice their thoughts while biting your tongue because you feel like their thoughts are not necessarily grounded in reality. When these conversations come about, I want to remind you that this is even more reason why they require real-life experiences. It's ironic how often I hear moms talk about how they struggle with their child's thoughts or opinions on topics they have little experience with. Yet, they don't give them the opportunity to gain that experience.

As annoying as the need to adjust the course of action is, this mommy superpower will serve you well when your child comes home from college on breaks. At times, it feels like you have just started to adapt to them being away at school, and then, before you know it, they are home visiting. You may think, "I am so glad you're home . . . !" And . . . "Who are you?" There can be an intense mix of emotions as their presence changes the household dynamic, and you begin to see some of the shifts they are making to figure out

who they are and where they belong. Be patient with yourself when you have these conflicting emotions. It's okay,
and it's part of the growth process—for everyone involved.
You will have moments where you are in love all over again
and other times when you think, "Haven't we been over
this a million times that you need to clean up after yourself?" This is all totally normal. I encourage you to sit back
and observe all the emotions you experience each time
there is a transition in your household. Take notes, keep a
journal, and talk to a therapist. Regardless of what method
works for you, it will help you to see what's working and
what isn't. For your own health, I also suggest you find
the things you enjoy doing—with and without your children—to take a breath during the transition. Grounding
during any transition is essential, especially for your sanity.

Speaking of transitions . . . this can also be a time in
our lives when our parents begin to require more of our
assistance. I have heard this time referred to as "the sand-
wich generation" because we are simultaneously caring for
our children and our aging parents. This period looks different for each person depending on your parents' age, if
they are still living, and if you are connected with them.
The stress of managing the emotions of your family, as well
as the logistics of aging parents, can feel heavy at times. I
have learned that the importance of fine-tuning all of the
skills discussed in earlier chapters comes to the forefront in
these times. Granted, we will continue to refine our tool-
box as the years go by, but if we haven't worked on our

skill-building early on in motherhood, it can become more challenging as our children age, and we must balance other needs.

FOOD FOR THOUGHT

- Remember congruence with your words and your behaviors.

- Reassess your values.

- Listen to your gut.

- Less is more when it comes to your opinion.

- The fear is real, the feeling is strong, and the love will remain.

- Make a pie chart of where your time is spent and write the percentage of time you spend in each category in the pieces of pie. Once you see this, you can decide how to split the pie differently.

- Reconnect with friends in your life.

- Don't take your child's decisions or path in life so personally.

- Be adaptable.

- I encourage you to observe all the emotions you experience each time there is a transition in your household. Take notes, keep a journal, or talk to a therapist.

- Consistently assess your preconceived assumptions.

MOTHERHOOD DAILY CHECKLIST

1. Are my partner and I on the same page about how to support our children in launching?
2. Are my partner and I having open and honest discussions about our finances?
3. Am I taking an honest motherhood self-inventory?
4. Am I taking time to cultivate other fulfilling relationships in my life?
5. How am I doing in terms of balancing my needs?

Question to Moms: *How do you balance your roles as a mom, daughter, colleague, etc.?*

"Is this even possible? Something always goes . . . I can't do it all. The biggest struggle is learning to let some things go and be okay with it. Also . . . leaning on my village is key."

―――――

"I made time to have a date night with my husband, and we were fortunate to have childcare. I find time to switch off with my husband to have breaks, and to make time for self-care. I have been told that I haven't changed since I became a mother, and I believe part of that is because I made time for my friends."

―――――

"This is the hardest part! I try my best, day after day, and realize I can't give everyone my one hundred percent. I sometimes feel like I'm not doing enough, but at the same time, I feel like I am doing my best."

———

"By being very organized."

———

"Balance? That's funny . . ."

———

"Very precariously. Sometimes, I feel like I'm not balancing it all that well. Something always takes a back seat because I can't do it all."

———

"I don't. If one thing gets all of my attention, then everything else suffers. Work and my son get all of my attention."

———

"I did it all; my sisters and I got together a lot with the kids, and my mother was supportive. It challenged my marriage, and our marriage suffered from having a child because we didn't talk about it. He would undermine and reprimand me in front of our daughter with everything. We didn't do well balancing, didn't feel supported and tried to do everything, and we didn't communicate or redefine roles. There's a reason I don't work: my marriage struggled, and I moved next to my parents."

"I was fortunate that, financially, I did not need to work. When you are in the throes of having small children, and with my husband being a police officer, my friendships overall took a back seat and became more occasional until later on because motherhood is so incredibly busy. I didn't feel 'pulled' because my husband was appreciative for all that I did and did not put any further demands on me, and I didn't put further demands upon him."

————

"From a young age, I knew that time is essential when wearing so many hats—i.e., mom, wife, daughter, and grandma. It is why I spent that time with those people in my life, which positively impacted my relationships."

————

"Balance is key in life. I learned to be centered in my God and follow the Flow. This has evolved over time. For years, I tried to do it all and found little was done to my best or left me depleted."

Action Step

How are you balancing all of your roles as your child grows? Is there an area you can work on to support better balance moving forward, and what does that look like?

Notes

CHAPTER 6

WHO AM I?

Stage 6–Readjusting When Your Children Move Out

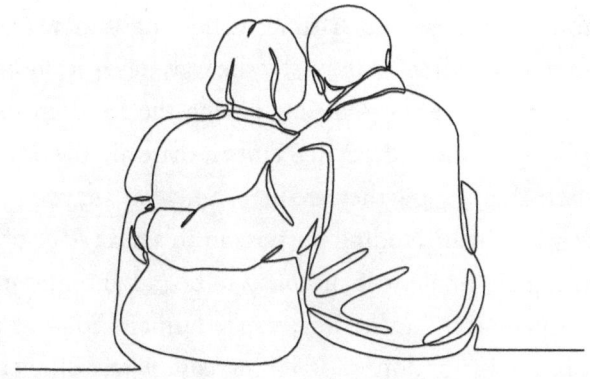

Who am I? This is a powerful question that we often ask ourselves at this stage in motherhood. It can be extremely scary to ask this question, as everything we thought gave us purpose in life is now changing. Many feel that being a mother gave them the purpose they longed for in life, more so than their career. When coming into this stage, there are pangs of "Was I a good mom?" "How badly did I emotionally damage my kids?" "Will my partner still want to be with me?" "Do I even like who I've become?" We begin to grapple with these powerful emotions while tearing down our walls. Think about it: As a mother, how many times over your lifetime were you asked to make plans, and you came up with an excuse to cancel, directly blaming your children? Please don't lie; we all have. Being a mother defines fundamental aspects of ourselves. It can also be a convenient "out" when we don't have the courage to set our own boundaries. Feeling lost at this stage is undeniably familiar, yet uncomfortable—no question.

You've spent so much time wondering and worrying about your children—which, by the way, never really ends; it just changes shape—to now having the freedom to do you. How freeing is that? Remember, these are the days we *dreamed* about. Now they are here. So, what are you going to do with them? Finding purpose in this next stage of life is freeing if you allow it. It's okay to be sad and grieve the loss of parenting in this way; you're human. You can also bask in the joy of doing something completely different if you so choose. Now, I know you're thinking, "Yeah, sure, I just go out and find a new purpose . . . that's not real!" I agree; it's not realistic to think it will happen overnight. I encourage people to engage in the things that make them feel good when they finish them. Start with something simple. Like everything else, this is a process—so what's the rush? Take your time, experiment, explore, and allow your-self to become captivated by what you stumble upon. I think that's the best thing we can do: be curious. Take the time to allow yourself freedom of thought. We often confine ourselves by thinking we can't do things and end up in a box of our own creation. This is a time to step outside of the box, no matter how uncomfortable it may be, and do it. It's okay to get lost.

My work with Megan is a perfect example of this process. Throughout our time together, she would discuss how lost she felt as her youngest of three had moved out to start her first job after college. We explored all of the emotions that she had experienced at this stage, from feeling lost, sad, grief-stricken, excited, confused, and fearful. In doing a deep dive, by allowing her to feel and express these emotions, we uncovered that being a mother is the only thing she has ever felt confident doing. We discussed how she was a truly good mom and how she felt in her element when in that role. We explored the other things in her life that make her feel confident—or areas she was willing to work on to build more confidence. As she gained more clarity, we explored what steps she was willing to take to try something she used to love to see if she still enjoyed the activity. We also discussed that starting with things she loves would help her get her bearings before she steps outside of her comfort zone to try something new. As we went through this process, she also realized that she felt highly uncomfortable having so much time to consider her own needs. We then examined how she could balance this out within her marriage and consider her husband's needs as well, as this would be the perfect opportunity to begin their reconnection process.

At this time in our lives, just as we see with Megan's journey, not only are we reflecting upon ourselves and our lives, but we are also reflecting upon our relationship with our partner. Some view this as a daunting task. They think, "Uh-oh . . . I don't know if I like my partner anymore," while others take this opportunity as, "Wow, this is great! We get to start dating and learning about each other all over again!" No matter how you look at this chapter in your life, it's new and requires further adaptation. Yes, I know . . . as if you haven't had to adapt to enough already. Fear of the unknown may arise within these questions, encompassing insecurity and angst. The number of thoughts going through our minds about where we are headed and what we want can be overwhelming. After all, when was the last time you were able to think about what you wanted and were able to execute it? It's likely years, at best.

With this thought comes great freedom while a slight layer of fear creeps in. At one point in our motherhood, our jobs seemed so straightforward: just get through the day and don't kill your children or partner. I'm kidding, of course, but as we moms know, things can get pretty challenging sometimes. Now, we are faced with the time and ability to think about ourselves, all while feeling like we don't know how to do that anymore. So what do we do with this freedom? We grab it and don't let it go! We take time each morning to read a chapter of *The Gut Check: How to*

Reconnect with Your Intuition and start tuning into what we need so we can begin fulfilling those needs (yes, that was a shameless plug for my last book). We write bucket lists and start creating ways and means to make each item on the list happen. Then, we find someone in our lives who will hold us accountable for doing them. We get out in nature and take walks, listen to music, swim, and have coffee dates with friends. We might take a class on something we have always wished to learn.

Please understand that it may feel uncomfortable to do all of this. It goes against what you have needed to do as a mother for many years. When that discomfort sets in, allow it. Don't try to avoid, escape, or ignore; it will only get louder. When we make too many changes too fast, we tend to resort to our old way of functioning because it's familiar. Observing yourself throughout this process is critical so you don't send yourself backward at a time when you can move forward by leaps and bounds.

This is also when we realize that our children don't have to like us. As harsh as that may sound, there is some truth to it. We recognize that as they enter young adulthood, we have diminished our influence over their chosen path—or how often we see or hear from them. Thinking about how our ability to influence them has decreased can be scary. Often, we can find ourselves not knowing how to walk this line. Other times, we fear saying something wrong and making our child angry. We may inadvertently push them away because they need space to regroup. This is like slow torture to most of us. We don't know how to adapt to our children's ongoing maturation process and tend to question ourselves each step of the way . . .

Am I saying too much?

Is this okay?

Do I call enough?

Do I call too much?

Am I annoying them?

The questions we ask ourselves can go on for days if we allow it. Isn't it funny how much we worry, yet most of us never talk to our kids about this? Why is that? I think the best thing we can do for our growing relationship with our young adult children is to have these wonderful, vulnerable conversations with them so we can all grow *together*. I know this isn't rocket science, but it is an idea most moms are scared to death to try. While managing this fear, we also realize that we have very little control or influence over how much they tell us—if anything at all—about their lives. Feeling this lack of control can be arduous as it can create fear while we wonder if they are okay, but we have nothing to go on.

The next part is challenging. What happens is our child starts dating someone seriously that we are not a fan of. Maybe we feel they are not the best match. What are we supposed to do at that point? Seeing our child fall in love with someone who we feel is unsuitable can be incredibly scary. But who are we to judge? Is it truly our place to provide our opinion? No, it's not. But deep within the recesses of our minds, we think that because we gave birth to these fabulous beings, we are entitled to have a say. I can tell you that you need to exercise discernment as to whether or not you should keep your mouth shut if you don't like who they have chosen. If your child is making choices that threaten their safety and mental health, clearly finding healthy ways to discuss this with them is critical. Yet if your child is making erroneous choices (in your eyes) about what they wear or how they style their hair, I strongly suggest you keep it to yourself.

So here's the hard truth: You take a significant risk in telling your child how you feel regarding specific areas of their lives, such as when they are in love. In sharing too much of how you think about their partner, you risk losing them or possibly changing your relationship with them. Keeping quiet, when appropriate, feels so wrong at times. But remember, when they are out on their own, they can do whatever they want. Open lines of communication will save you at this stage—and every other stage, for that matter. Keep listening and encouraging them to talk while keeping your opinions to yourself unless asked.

As we see our children beginning to cultivate their lives in a way that feels good for them, we realize that we can think about potential retirement or partial retirement and how our finances are shifting. Seeing our children move out and create their lives is tremendously joyful while at the same time showing us that we may be able to consider this new chapter in our lives in a more profound way.

What does retirement mean, and how do I want that to look? Do I even want to retire? Do I have the resources to retire? Retirement is something that looks different for everyone, and it has many variables that require thoughtful planning. Taking the time to talk with your partner about what you want and what your financial picture looks like is extremely helpful. Finances are a finicky thing, and some couples plan their future finances starting early in their relationship, while others may only have the resources to do so later in life. Regardless of when you are able to put money away for your future, it would be best if you did it.

Food for Thought

- Find things you enjoy.
- Be curious about yourself and your life.
- Read *The Gut Check: How to Reconnect with your Intuition*.
- Write a bucket list.
- Have vulnerable conversations with your children about communication and boundaries.
- Plan for your future.

MOTHERHOOD DAILY CHECKLIST

1. How am I making strides to find purpose?
2. What am I doing to reconnect with myself?

3. What am I doing to reconnect with my spouse on a deeper level?
4. How am I managing my discomfort when trying new things?
5. Am I being judgmental of my child's choices or the choices of those around me?

Question to Moms: *What do you find most challenging about being a mom?*

"Most challenging: Not letting mom guilt get me all the time! And letting go . . ."

———

"I felt like my freedom was taken from me. When I wasn't with them, I was always thinking about my children. However, I was fortunate I had children."

———

"Our children learned to separate from us; however, my phone was always on in case they needed me."

———

"I would find parenting with my husband challenging, and finding ways to communicate more effectively was challenging. I found that I was always exhausted mentally, emotionally, and physically during the early stage of their development."

"I was constantly dealing with my kids, fighting with one another, and trying to stay calm."

———

"Dealing with other moms, having difficult conversations—drugs, sex, intimacy, friendships."

———

"Constantly second-guessing myself and if I am raising sociopaths or decent humans."

———

"There's nothing that you can do when you are sad, mad, or anxious; you still have to parent. There is little space for you to give attention to your own space because your child always needs you."

———

"Disciplining my child—enforcing it consistently. If you're not consistent, you're screwed. I feel everyone should take a class in parenting."

———

"Watching my kids struggle."

———

"The most challenging thing about being a mom is losing touch with yourself."

———

"Having all of my preconceived notions put to the test, about how this would go. It was never as simple as I thought it was."

———

"The most challenging aspect for me about being a mom is knowing that I cannot protect my children, especially adult children. They are no longer my responsibility, and to know they go through struggles is—and will always be—frustrating, because it is their responsibility to care for themselves."

———

"The most challenging part of being a mother was separating myself from others' opinions and judgments regarding my choices as a mother, and my children's choices."

Action Step

What have you found most challenging about being a mom up to this point, and why?

Notes

_____
_____
_____
_____
_____
_____
_____
_____
_____
_____
_____
_____
_____
_____
_____
_____
_____
_____
_____
_____
_____
_____
_____
_____
_____

CHAPTER 7

PARENTING AND GRANDPARENTING...
COMING FULL CIRCLE

Stage 7–When Our Children Have Children

The joy of simply allowing yourself to enjoy your grand-children is truly a gift. The beauty of this gift lies in the fact that you are no longer charged with the responsibility of teaching them; instead, you have the freedom to simply love them. You can serve as a grounding force for your children while offering unconditional love to your grandchildren. By being that stable presence, you support your children in becoming the best parents they can be, all while reinforcing their values. You now have access to wisdom that may have eluded you when you were a young mother, as you were often weighed down by a plethora of emotions. This sense of freedom now empowers you to support your children fully and wholeheartedly as they navigate the bumpy terrain of parenting. Be the person you needed when you first became a mother. There's something to be said for the gifts that come with age.

As we find ourselves crawling on the floor with our grandchildren, we are reminded of our physical limitations. Focusing on health and wellness, which may have been neglected in our younger years, plays a key role in how fully we can engage with our grandchildren. This stage of life offers a beautiful opportunity to nourish and respect our bodies in ways we might not have before. Being a grandmother comes with the wisdom of time itself. You are more acutely aware of time's finite nature and its preciousness. This deeper understanding helps you truly appreciate and cherish each moment you have on this earth. Some lessons can only be learned with the passage of time, and that is the essence of wisdom. It's something earned through experience, and it's a treasure we can pass on to our grandchildren and future generations—if they are willing to listen.

As mothers, we often believe we're invincible, even when we don't feel that way. We want to believe we can do it all, see it all, and heal it all. But at this stage of life, we come to realize that our resources—both physical and emotional—are limited. Taking care of ourselves is no longer just a luxury; it's a necessity that can determine the difference between life and death. It's crucial to be mindful of how we spend our time and energy, as we discussed in the exercise with Janet earlier. In this light, it's essential to get clear on how we want to show up for ourselves, our children, and our grandchildren.

Ask yourself: Do you want to be "Grandma Daycare" or simply "Grandma"? Spending time with your grandchildren is wonderful, and the desire to help your children is strong. We know how challenging raising a family can be, and we naturally want to ease their stress however we can. But make sure that it's not at your own expense. Remember, this is a time in your life when the "I have to" list is small, and the "I want to" list is long. Standing in your power is essential. Don't let guilt take over anymore—this is your time to embrace the freedom you've earned, so embrace it.

Now, let's say you decide to help your children by watching your grandchildren from time to time. The issue you may face is staying in the role of grandma, not stepping back into the role of mom. We must respect how our children choose to raise their own kids. Yes, we often feel like we have all the answers and know what's best, but our children may strongly disagree. Our job at this stage is to give them the space to be the parents they want to be, not the parents we think they should be. By doing so, we show them that we believe in their abilities. We also prove, once again, that we can keep our opinions to ourselves. I know it's exhausting, but I also know that everyone benefits when we're mindful of our words and use them sparingly. Just when you thought you were free to speak your mind, you realize that maintaining balance is still necessary. That balance means saving your opinions for the times when your children ask for them.

I have to give credit to my own mother. Time and time again, she has held her tongue in situations where I know she had strong opinions she was eager to share—but she didn't. She's mastered the art of thinking before speaking, a skill I'm still working on. This skill is especially useful when navigating relationships with in-laws, particularly daughters-in-law. The stereotype of the overbearing, nosy, pushy, and intrusive mother-in-law is all too familiar. And yet, there's little acknowledgment that without your mother-in-law, you wouldn't have met your partner. Think about that for a moment. Given the stigma, the relationship between mother-in-law and daughter-in-law can feel fraught from the beginning. We enter into it with the hope of being close and connected but with the wisdom to know that things can get tricky if we don't mind our "p's" and "q's." This relationship becomes even more delicate when grandchildren enter the picture. At this stage, every grandmother is aware of the power her daughter-in-law holds. Depending on the relationship, there may be a fear about managing things in a way that doesn't result in limited time or connection with your grandchildren. This reality reinforces the need to tread carefully and be mindful.

As we practice mindfulness, it's important to check in with ourselves about letting go. Letting go of our preconceived notions of how life was supposed to look, how our relationships with our children and loved ones would be, or how we expected to feel at this point in time. This stage of life offers the opportunity to release some of the responsibilities we've carried for years and allow our children to step up. Maybe you're tired of cooking Easter brunch—so let it go. Maybe cooking one more meal feels exhausting—you're allowed to feel that way, and you're allowed to ask your children if they'd like to invite you over for dinner. This is a time to learn how to receive. Many adult children want the chance to give back to their parents, and as parents, we should allow them that joy.

Health issues arise, friends and partners are lost, and we must learn to ask for support. The earlier we start this process, the easier it will be to ask for help in the later stages of life. While I don't want to sound morbid, this stage of life brings us face-to-face with our mortality. No, we're not like cartons of milk with an expiration date, but we do have a finite amount of time in these bodies. With that knowledge comes amazing things, like the awareness that there's more out there than what we see before us. The idea that this is all there is becomes too much to bear, and our desire to believe in something bigger grows stronger, knocking on our door more frequently.

As we slow down in life, we often sit in self-reflection regarding how we have spent our life, what we have done, and how we feel about it as a collective. Our frame of reference shrinks as the ones we love start to pass or become ill. With each death, there is a hole in our hearts that becomes increasingly difficult to fill. The grief of loss intensifies the more we lose longtime friends who share our frame of reference and life stories. And then, there's the unimaginable grief of losing a child. While this can happen at any age, the longer we live, the more likely it seems. This fear plagues us throughout our years of raising children, and it can intensify as our children grow older and face aging themselves.

It is in these moments that we need to seek connection on a deeper level.

Knowing what you know now, how do you use that information to inform the way you choose to live the rest of your days? What a powerful question and a fantastic position to be in. Divorce yourself from the "old ways" of being and thinking, and allow yourself the space to be who you were put on this earth to be. The only limits you now face are the ones you've placed on yourself. Those who live the longest are often the ones who have managed to free themselves from their own constraints.

Take Maryanne, for example. When she first came to see me, she was seventy-five years old and had just lost her husband. Before his death, she had already lost several friends, leaving her feeling as though her world was rapidly shrinking. The loss of her husband was traumatic, to say the least. They had been together for many years, and she spoke often of how deeply in love they remained despite the difficulties they had faced in their marriage. During our sessions, I came to understand how Maryanne viewed life, even through her profound grief. We explored how, despite her sorrow, she allowed herself to fully feel each emotion and let it pass, fully embracing the wisdom of the phrase "This, too, shall pass."

Over time, I realized that Maryanne wasn't necessarily seeking my help in the traditional sense. She simply needed someone to share her stories with—stories of her life and the joy she had experienced with those she loved. By walking alongside her in her grief, I was able to offer her a space where she felt seen and heard, nurtured, and free to tell her story. Later in our work together, I asked her to write her obituary. Her initial reaction was, "Jess, that sounds awful!" But as we explored her discomfort, she articulated that she was afraid that writing her obituary would somehow cause her death. I explained to her that this exercise wasn't about death itself but the emotions it stirred and the healing that could come from facing those feelings.

I'd love to explore this concept of release with you further as you come to the end of this book: that is, releasing the emotions tied to the aging process. At different points in our lives, the reality of our age can sneak up on us, whether it's when we catch a glimpse of ourselves in the mirror or in the unflattering lighting of a dressing room. We might think, "That's not me!" But I encourage you to hold onto how you feel and let go of your expectations of how you believe you are "supposed to" look.

I recall watching an episode of *Grace and Frankie* where they talked about how, after a certain age, you become invisible. I want to challenge that idea. Invisible to whom? I've met women in their later years who are more vibrant and full of life than women half their age. Just because your body isn't what it used to be doesn't mean you aren't seen. I see you, and I thank you for showing others what it means to age with grace and dignity. We don't need cosmetic surgery to appear younger; the most beautiful women I know are those with wrinkles and scars, unafraid to share the stories they tell.

As we enter this final chapter of life, it's okay to feel tired at times and to come to terms with accepting death rather than fearing it. Some women grow tired and feel lonely as their inner circles dwindle to just a few loved ones. Others continue to embrace life with an untouchable zest, welcoming their age and wisdom. Wherever you find yourself on this spectrum, reflecting on your feelings about mortality can be helpful for both you and your loved ones.

As we age, our children may start to fear that our time is limited. Each child may react to this in their own way, but I believe it's crucial that we, as the leaders of our families, create space for this conversation. These discussions can be profoundly healing, allowing us to process our emotions and fears together. By being vulnerable with our children, we show them that it's okay—that we are not afraid of what's to come. We can also use these moments to share our wishes for them after we pass and discuss the arrangements we've put in place.

One piece of sage advice I'd like to offer is to make your passing as logistically simple as possible. When someone we love dies, we're thrown, knee-deep, into unfamiliar emotional territory while simultaneously being expected to handle logistics we may know nothing about. Take the time to face what's ahead and clearly spell everything out in your will for your loved ones. This will give you a sense of peace, knowing that when the time comes, they'll be able to grieve without added stress.

Final Thoughts

- Care for your body—it's the home of your soul.

- Be intentional with how you spend your time and energy.

- Embrace simplicity; sometimes less truly is more.

- Align your daily actions with your core values.

- Consider the legacy you want to leave behind—are you using your time to build it?

- Write your obituary as an exercise in reflecting on how you want to be remembered.

- Accept and honor the natural changes in your body as you age.

MOTHERHOOD DAILY CHECKLIST

1. Am I choosing my words with care and intention?
2. What kind of legacy do I want to leave behind?
3. Am I allowing acceptance and grace into my life?
4. What do I need to let go of today?
5. If I died tomorrow, would I feel at peace? If not, what changes can I make now?

Question to Moms: *What do you love about being a mom —at any stage of motherhood?*

"Watching them turn into themselves . . . I love seeing them do what they love and learning from *them*. That's really cool too."

———

"I love that every day is different; I love that my children teach me something new every day, they challenge me, and they teach me to be a better person. I always wanted to be a mother and I am grateful for my children."

———

"I love the feeling of unconditional love, watching them learn new things or accomplish something, being able to do fun kid activities, and of course the endless snacks!"

———

"I love all of it; I love being needed."

———

"I love watching the people that they are becoming, their personalities and characteristics; how they interact with their friends."

———

"I love how spontaneous it can be and how playful it makes me feel. Just the experience of love in its purest form."

———

"The companionship, watching her grow, teaching her new things."

———

"I love everything about it, loved being a part of their lives—I was a mother that celebrated everything."

———

"The cuddles! The love; deep talks, and the excitement of new discoveries about my son."

———

"I love all of it. I love the diversity it brings to your life, the different personalities, the paths and roles your children take, the professions they choose. You are living vicariously, in some regards, as your children shape their lives. It's always a learning experience."

"I love that tiny human beings came from me and that I love them unconditionally and I have shown them to love unconditionally."

———

"What I love about being a mother is being a close observer of each of my children and praying for them to follow their true path. I love seeing their lives unfold as they discover their true identity."

Action Step

I want you to think about what *you* love about being a mom. Take the time to write your thoughts.

Final Thoughts for Moms Who Have Adult Children and Grandchildren

Asking questions of mothers of all ages and walks of life was extremely interesting. Some answered the questions in person, some over the phone, and others asked to have time to think about the questions and respond via email. What I found extremely interesting is that there appeared to be a guilt that arose when they felt they were answering the questions too honestly or in a way that someone would judge their answer. The questions that appeared to trigger the most emotion were about what was challenging about being a mom or balancing your roles. For those who had spent time doing their own emotional work and introspection at different points in their lives, being honest with themselves appeared to come a little easier. Other women struggled to express their true feelings for fear of being viewed as a "bad mom." Our culture tends to come with pressures to love being a mother, and if you don't, then something is "wrong with you."

What also became clearer when asking women who had children and grandchildren was that the further you are away from parenting, the more you look back upon your parenting experience through a positive lens. I don't know whether it's the beauty of how menopause impacts our memory or how we reflect upon our lives, but it appears that where we are as mothers in the parenting process plays a significant role in how we view our role and in what light. On the contrary, I noticed that the moms who answered the above questions in the early stages of motherhood (stages 1 and 2) were in the depths of no sleep and feeling pulled in all directions while wanting to be left alone at times. These women often felt as though their exhaustion would never end, and they couldn't see any light; at times, it sounded like their husbands didn't either. It quickly became clear that everyone has their sweet spot in mothering. For some, they loved the infancy stage and their child needing them for everything, while others shined brighter during the teenage years. The experience was different for each mom, and many factors played a role in this experience. No two experiences are the same, but there are some commonalities from which we can grow.

Regardless of their mothering experience, what I loved about asking these questions is that women wanted to answer them to help other women. This was beautiful in so many ways. When hearing that I was writing a book about being a mom, women were enthusiastic about expressing themselves and had a strong desire to contribute whatever wisdom they could for those mothers out there who need support for whatever reason.

The biggest takeaway I have seen is that the better you care for yourself at the beginning of your motherhood experience, the better you will adapt and rebalance as life takes its turns. When women put all their eggs in one basket, such as focusing solely on raising their children at the expense of their marriage or just focusing on their career at the expense of their children and husband, they face more profound challenges in later parenting stages.

An interesting caveat to caring for yourself as a mom is all the cultural pressure in roles that come into play. In talking with moms from different generations, it appears that there is resentment among mothers toward their partners of younger generations (Millennials and below) around having to work but feeling like they are still expected to maintain all things "mom" related. When speaking to women in the Baby Boomer generation, even though women worked, there was still more societal grace and importance placed on mothers being able to stay with their children if they chose to create a solid foundation for their families.

I have noticed that with mothers of younger generations, there are fewer women who have a choice to work due to our economic realities. When women perceive this choice to be taken away from them, there is some resentment toward their partner around the roles they wish to take on. The societal matrix that we are currently experiencing surrounding the navigation of roles within partnerships can be highly taxing. More and more mothers are expected to work—or we realize we want to work—and yet, at the same time, the messaging is to make sure we are not emasculating our partners when it comes to household earning power or the division of labor within the home. How confusing . . . We are often expected to work because the ability to live on a single income and raise a family is increasingly more difficult. Yet, if we make too much money, it can make our partners feel insecure. We may become resentful that we do so and concurrently do the lion's share of the care for our children. Of course, there are exceptions, but it is a prevailing theme.

So what gives? I genuinely have no idea. It seems that the family system as a whole is going through a significant shift. Therefore, having healthy discussions with our partners about our roles within the family system is essential. Ultimately, as long as we are on the same page in our partnerships, it doesn't matter what the cultural or societal norms are; we need to be in agreement and feel good as individuals and as a team. Yes, you got it . . . communication is crucial. And making sure that your decisions—as a team—feel like a win for both parties is the secret sauce.

Notes

AFTERWORD

In the time it has taken to speak to moms from all walks of life and write this book, I have been given the gift of deeper connection. This gift has also highlighted the connection we need and are missing in our society as mothers. We need to lift the veil around motherhood and connect around all facets of our journey, not just the ones that we think we "should" be able to discuss. Our need for reassurance and validation that we are doing a good job is genuine and doesn't make us weak.

Taking time to care for our health and wellness is essential for the longevity we seek. I've learned that if we don't take care of ourselves consistently throughout this experience, we take significant risks of suffering medical and emotional consequences from our own neglect. I would love your help in spreading compassion to all mothers you encounter. Show them that you see them, hear them, and support them. Let's use this book as a tool to open up the dialogue and build stronger foundations within our relationships. The healthier we are, the better we will make this world for our families.

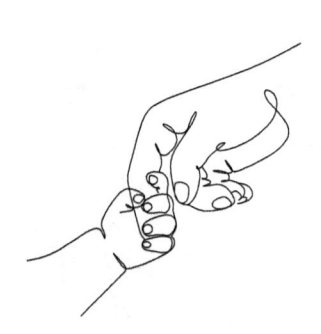